Twayne's English Authors Series

EDITOR OF THIS VOLUME

Bertram H. Davis

The Florida State University

JUNIUS
AND
PHILIP FRANCIS

TEAS 259

Philip Francis

JUNIUS and
PHILIP FRANCIS

By DAVID McCRACKEN

University of Washington

TWAYNE PUBLISHERS
A DIVISION OF G. K. HALL & CO., BOSTON

Copyright © 1979 by G. K. Hall & Co.

Published in 1979 by Twayne Publishers,
A Division of G. K. Hall & Co.
All Rights Reserved

Printed on permanent/durable acid-free paper and bound
in the United States of America

First Printing

Library of Congress Cataloging in Publication Data

McCracken, David.
Junius and Philip Francis.

(Twayne's English authors series ; TEAS 259)
Bibliography: p. 149–52
Includes index.
1. Junius, pseud., author of the "Letters".
2. Great Britain—Politics and government—1760–1820.
3. Francis, Philip, 1708?–1773. I. Title.
DA508.A5M3   1979   320.9'41'073   78-21045
ISBN 0-8057-6753-3

For
My Father and Mother

Contents

About the Author

David McCracken was born and raised in Kentucky, took his B.A. (1961) at Oberlin College and his M.A. (1962) and Ph.D. (1966) in English at the University of Chicago. He has taught at Alice Lloyd College (in Pippa Passes, Kentucky), the University of Chicago, and now teaches at the University of Washington, where he is an Associate Professor. He has served for two years there as Director of English Graduate Studies. His publications include an edition of William Godwin's novel, *Caleb Williams,* containing for the first time the original ending of the novel. In addition, he has written a number of reviews and articles on eighteenth-century English literature, including studies of Godwin, Edmund Burke, and Samuel Johnson.

Preface

The title of this study — *Junius and Philip Francis* — indicates that the subject is both single and double. Philip Francis and Junius are a single historical person, yet during the years 1768–72, Junius, as Francis' rhetorical creation, had an existence of his own, an existence not even tentatively linked to Francis until four decades later. The identity of Junius was a profound secret in the eighteenth century, much debated in the nineteenth, and, some will insist, not beyond all doubt today. The link between the two has in fact been convincingly confirmed by Alvar Ellegard in *Who Was Junius?* (1962). In a sense, however, the secret nature of Junius will exist as long as his name. In his three years of malicious political invective, he possessed a brilliance, awesomeness, and mystery that Philip Francis could never publicly equal. Francis, in his career as civil servant, councillor in India, respected political writer, and member of Parliament, led a full life and had no small impact on his age, as the careers of Warren Hastings and Edmund Burke amply witness. But from a historical and literary perspective, Junius is nonetheless the more important, more interesting figure; or, to put it another way, Philip Francis' private, secret self is more interesting and more important historically than Philip Francis' public, official self.

The focus of this study, then, is primarily on Junius as a creation of Philip Francis and as a phenomenon of his age. There has been very little serious critical discussion of the literary and historical aspects of Junius, although not because he has been ignored. On the contrary, W. E. H. Lecky maintained in the late nineteenth century that "probably no English book, except the plays of Shakespeare, has been submitted to such a minute and exhaustive criticism as *The Letters of Junius*."[1] The problem is that this mass of writing is almost exclusively concerned with the question, Who was Junius? The question was pursued so ardently by literary historians, amateurs, and cranks that it eventually became a crashing bore, which partly explains, I suspect, why there has been relatively little written on Junius in the twentieth century. Thanks to Dr. Ellegard's distinguished and careful work, the question is now solved, the corpus of

Junian writings is now established for the first time, and we are free to pursue other questions about him.

I have therefore organized this book around the ideas and rhetoric of Junius in the context of their era, of their impact then and later, and of Francis' other writings. Chapter 1 sketches the literary and historical context of the Junius letters as a certain kind of political writing, adapted by Francis to the new medium of the newspaper in order to achieve the maximum political effect. Chapter 2 surveys the attempts to pierce the mystery of Junius' identity — the wild speculations, the skeptical criticisms, and the gradual accumulation of circumstantial evidence which identifies Junius with Francis. The next three chapters examine Junius' involvement in the crucial political issues of his time and his attempts to affect those issues through the power of his pen: his writings on the constitutional crisis over Wilkes and the Middlesex election, his attacks on King George III and his ministers, and his struggle for freedom of the press. On the basis of Junius' stands on the topical issues which evoked his satire, chapter 6 proceeds to a consideration of his political philosophy; the letters, Junius claimed, contain "principles worthy to be transmitted to posterity." The topical political stands and their underlying principles, however, are all modified by Junius' rhetorical task of persuading his readers to believe and act in certain ways. His strategies of persuasion — including his assumed character, his treatment of the audience, his style, his arrangement, and his choice of arguments — constitute the subject of chapter 7. The later writings of Francis — Junius unmasked — are surveyed in chapter 8.

A version of chapter 6 has been printed by *Enlightenment Essays*. I wish to thank the interlibrary loan staff at the University of Washington for obtaining a number of rare pamphlets, the National Portrait Gallery in London for permission to reproduce Francis' portrait for the frontispiece, Julie Schairer for typing the manuscript, and Karl Sifferman and my wife for their help in the final stages.

Chronology

1740   Philip Francis born in Dublin, October 22.

1751   Moves to England for education.

1756   Becomes junior clerk in secretary of state's office.

1758   Goes to France on military expedition as secretary to General Edward Bligh.

1760   Appointed secretary to Lord Kinnoul's embassy to Portugal.

1761–
1762   Amanuensis to William Pitt (later Lord Chatham).

1762   Marries Elizabeth Macrabie against the wishes of both families. Appointed first clerk in the War Office.

1768   General election; beginning of Wilkes controversy over Middlesex election. Chatham resigns. Junius' first letter (uncollected).

1769   January 21, Letter I of the collected letters appears. December 19, Junius' "Address to the King."

1770   January, Grafton ministry replaced by Lord North.

1771–
1772   Junius corresponds privately with John Wilkes.

1772   January 21, Junius' last letter; January–March, Veteran letters. March, Francis resigns from War Office. March 3, authorized collection of Junius letters published by Woodfall.

1773   Appointed member of Bengal Council. Meets Clive and Burke.

1774   October, arrives in Calcutta and begins opposition to Warren Hastings at once.

1779   August, wounded in duel with Hastings.

1780   Leaves India.

1784–
1807   Member of Parliament for Yarmouth (Isle of Wight), 1784–90; for Bletchingley, 1790–96; for Appleby, 1802–7.

1787   *Observations on the Defence Made by Warren Hastings.*

1788–
1795   Assists in impeachment of Hastings.

1793   *Letter to Lord North* (composed in 1777).

1806 October, knighted by King George III, Order of the Bath.
1807 *Letter to Lord Howick.*
1810 *Reflections on Paper in Circulation.*
1814 Marries again, his first wife having died in 1806; presents bride with a copy of *Junius*. *Letter to Earl Grey.*
1818 *Historical Questions Exhibited.* Dies September 23.

CHAPTER 1

Introduction

I *History and Literature*

T HE truth is, that [the Junius letters] stand almost alone amongst satirical and logical productions in the possession of characteristics which belong to enduring literature. They can be read as history. Nay, more; the history of the time cannot be understood without them."[1] The verdict of a nineteenth-century historian sounds exaggerated in light of Junius' relative neglect in the twentieth century, but he has accurately identified the double appeal — history and literature — of Junius' letters. To Junius' contemporaries, however, the letters were neither history nor, in its limited sense, literature; they were polemical political writings about specific men and measures calculated to move readers to action. By virtue of their explicitness and their powerful effect, they have become history, relics of a past that is only partly recoverable but which we insist on trying to recover for its own interest and for the light it sheds on our own time. In addition to this, the excellence of style, the imaginative — not simply factual — treatment of men and measures, and the emotive power of the letters establish their literary superiority over writings of a similar kind. It is impossible now to view them as simply one or the other. If read as history without attention to their rhetorical and literary qualities, they will lead the reader woefully astray, for the portraits of Grafton and Bedford in the letters bear little resemblance to the actual men they represent. Like Aristophanes' rendering of Socrates suspended in a basket in the clouds, Junius' satiric portraits are attempts at artistic rather than literal truth. On the other hand, the artistry cannot exist or be perceived apart from the historical men, measures, and ideas that form the content of the letters. They are not belles lettres which create an imaginative world of their own.

13

The *Letters of Junius,* then, are best read as history-and-literature. They should be seen within their historical context — a context which was modified by the letters themselves, as Junius harassed the ministers, incited the opposition in Parliament to action, and aroused the passions of his readers — and, at the same time, they should be read with a literary sensitivity to the means by which Junius creates his effects as he tries to alter his political world.

Much literature of late eighteenth-century England is intellectual or polemical prose; it is clearly the greatest literary form in what is appropriately called the "Age of Johnson." There were, of course, notable achievements in other literary forms. Smollett and Sterne are among the best comic novelists in the language, though there were no other major novelists until Scott and Jane Austen at the beginning of the next century. The novel was an increasingly popular genre among readers, but in the second half of the century it consisted largely of sentimental, gothic, and propaganda fiction. There were notable poems, like Gray's *Elegy,* but Collins, Cowper, Chatterton, and Ossian do not approach the poetical genius of Pope just before or Blake and Wordsworth just after them. In the theater, there was no enduring tragedy and, with the important exception of Goldsmith and Sheridan, little but sentimental comedy or now-forgotten farce.

The achievement of the age in nonfiction prose, however, is prodigious. It seems that nearly every year saw the publication of some major, enduring prose work in history, travel, politics, philosophy, morality, natural history, economics, law, or biography. It is to this large body of "literature of experience," as opposed to "literature of imagination," that the Junius letters of 1768 to 1772 belong. There is, of course, a large body of such writing in any age, but in the late eighteenth century it is of remarkably high quality. Political polemics abound, but they are seldom of the caliber of Junius' letters. They are, as Coleridge said, "perfect in their kind."[2]

The same is true of many other types of nonfiction prose written during this age. Samuel Johnson was the most versatile writer among them, and indeed is among the greatest literary geniuses of England. His achievements in poetry, fiction, and editing need not be mentioned here; what is of more concern in this context is his literature which deals with literal truth, with the world of experience — his moral and critical essays in the *Rambler,*

Adventurer, and *Idler* (published in the 1750s), his *Dictionary of the English Language* (1755), his political pamphlets of the 1770s, his travel book, *Journey to the Western Islands of Scotland* (1775), his biographies and literary criticism in *Lives of the Poets* (1779-81), and his other critical essays, prayers, sermons, and legal writings. Furthermore, the half-century known as the Age of Johnson is filled with prose masterpieces by other writers: Hume's *Enquiry Concerning Human Understanding* (1748), *History of England* (1754-62), and *Dialogues Concerning Natural Religion* (1779); Burke's *Sublime and Beautiful* (1756), *Reflections on the Revolution in France* (1790), and many other essays; Goldsmith's histories, essays, and *Letters from a Citizen of the World* (1760-61); Blackstone's *Commentaries* (1765-69); Sir Joshua Reynolds' *Discourses on Art* (1769); Gibbon's *Decline and Fall of the Roman Empire* (1776); Adam Smith's *Wealth of Nations* (1776); Gilbert White's *Natural History of Selborne* (1789); Boswell's *Life of Samuel Johnson* (1791); Paine's *Rights of Man* (1791); Godwin's *Political Justice* (1793); and Malthus' *Essay on Population* (1798), to mention only a few of the important works. Junius was clearly in good company.

Such works as these attempt to deal with literal truths — the record of places, plants, or wildlife, the behavior of individuals, the events of history or of a particular man, the social and political actions of a people, the functioning of economic laws, the operation of the mind — and they ask to be judged accordingly. They do not try to construct an imagined world as a poem or novel does; instead they exist in a direct relation to what we see, feel, and know. Given the critical climate of opinion today, it is not always easy to consider this writing, with its often didactic quality and its focus on experience, as "literature." The Romantic era has left us with a strong notion of literature as the product of the isolated genius, creating imagined worlds, and the New Criticism of the twentieth century has directed our attention to the literary work as an artifact which exists in a world of images, metaphors, irony, symbols. Authors of late eighteenth-century prose literature, however, held widely different presuppositions. The artist was not a "maker" but a skilled craftsman dealing with literal truths to instruct and please his audience.

Yet in placing Junius in a literary context, it is not entirely sufficient to remark only on the intellectual and polemical prose tradition, of which he is clearly a part. It has already been mentioned

that much of Junius is not literally true at all; the portraits of
Grafton and Bedford are more creations than reports, and not
because Junius was a sloppy observer or a political madman. For
the reason behind such portraits we must turn to a second literary
tradition: that of Augustan satire.[3]

In Pope's *Epistle to Dr. Arbuthnot,* the satirist, plagued on all
sides by knaves and fools, issues his challenge to the world: "A lash
like mine no honest man shall dread, / But all such babbling block-
heads in his stead." Then begins his famous portrait of Sporus —
Lord John Hervey — "that thing of silk, / . . . that mere white
Curd of Ass's milk": "Yet let me flap this Bug with gilded wings, /
This painted Child of Dirt that stinks and stings." The ensuing
portrait brilliantly and maliciously portrays Sporus not as a
realistic, literal version of Lord Hervey, but as a metaphorical
representative of his specious beauty and real vileness — a "well-
bred Spaniel," "familiar Toad," "one vile Antithesis," "Eve's
Tempter." Sporus is not simply the literal Hervey but becomes, in
Maynard Mack's words, an *"exemplum* of radical Evil."[4]
Something similar happens in Junius' portraits of George III's ministers. Junius, like Pope, makes use of specific names and actual
facts in the portraits but he is not striving for a well-balanced,
literally true characterization of Grafton, Bedford, or Mansfield;
instead, they become types of evil which are corrupting the nation.
Many have accused Junius — and Pope — of inexcusable personal
malice, but such a charge misses the point. The literal truth of the
portraits is consciously sacrificed for the analogical truth of the
evil which they embody. Pope, like most writers of the
eighteenth century, deals with the here and now, with actual
experiences; hence his constant references to particular men,
places, and events of his day. But he transplants these into an
imaginative world, analogous to the world of experience but different. Lord Hervey becomes Sporus, "radical Evil," but at the
same time retains the fawning, mumbling, strutting character of
the actual Hervey.

Thus Junius, with his forthright political principles, his reasoned
analyses of political issues, and his seemingly inexhaustible knowledge of personal scandal, is no aberration in the eighteenth century:
he writes within the thriving context of a Johnsonian literature of
experience, at times eschewing literal truth for the imaginative
world of Augustan satire.

II   *The Medium*

The literary life of many eighteenth-century authors was closely connected with politics, as evidenced, for example, by Defoe's enormous political production, Swift's *Conduct of the Allies* and *Examiner,* Fielding's *Champion,* Smollett's *Briton,* Churchill's contributions to the *North Briton,* Johnson's *False Alarm* and *Patriot,* and Burke's writings, which are almost entirely political. The involvement ranged from scribbling for whatever faction could provide a handsome sum of money (as in the remarkable case of Defoe, who sometimes wrote for opposing factions at the same time), to supporting ministerial friends and seeking personal advancement (Swift), to writing as one facet of an active political life (Burke).

The most common vehicles for political writings were journals, periodical essays, pamphlets, and newspapers. The journals usually appeared once a week and contained an article on politics, literature, or manners, plus general news and advertisements. The most widely read periodical essays were the *Spectator, Tatler,* and *Rambler,* which usually avoided political subjects; the form, however, was often used for political purposes. On May 29, 1762, Smollett began a weekly ministerial paper called *The Briton* (so called because of George III's statement that he gloried "in the name of Briton"). To counter this political line, Wilkes launched his *North Briton* (alluding to the hated Scots) on June 5 as an anti-ministerial paper. Not to be outdone, the government responded with another weekly paper, *The Auditor,* begun by Arthur Murphy on June 10. Such papers were usually one-man operations, financed by the government or a wealthy opposition leader.

In the days of Defoe and Swift, the pamphlet was the usual medium for political controversy, and it remained important throughout the century. But by the 1760s, despite the *Critical Review*'s characterization of "this our pamphlet-loving age," the newspaper had become the most important vehicle for political writing. Horace Walpole took a dim view of this development. "The paper war," he wrote in 1763, "is rekindled with violence, but produces no wit; nay, scarce produces the bulk of a pamphlet, for the fashionable warfare at present is carried on by anonymous letters in the daily newspapers," and he later added that "it is certain that from this time, when anonymous writers could get their letters printed in the daily newspapers, pamphlets grew exceedingly more rare.'' [5] The warfare still involved paid political writers; the medium had simply changed.

Newspapers as we know them today are quite different from their eighteenth-century predecessors. The first London daily newspaper, the *Daily Courant,* appeared in 1702: it consisted of one folio page with two columns, and contained short paragraphs translated from foreign journals. From this beginning, newspapers multiplied and changed considerably. In 1730 the ''advertisers'' began. At first they contained only advertisements and were distributed free, but soon a few articles were added and they were sold for the same price as other newspapers. Shortly, all daily newspapers were ''advertisers.'' The *Public Advertiser* — in which the Junius letters appeared — was founded in 1734 as the *London Daily Post and General Advertiser* and assumed its more famous name in 1752. [6] In 1758, at the age of nineteen, Henry Sampson Woodfall became editor of the paper and made it into one of the great newspapers of the century. During the years of the Junius letters, the *Public Advertiser* contained a large number of advertisements, some general news, and, most interesting, letters from usually anonymous correspondents. There were no features, editorials, or opinion columns, as we know them. Therefore, the correspondence, especially when it reached the excellence and power of Junius' letters, was much more important and influential than the ''letters to the editor'' today. A more accurate analogy in today's press would be the editorial or leader.

By 1760 London had eighty-six newspapers — not all of them daily — and, like today, many people felt that they could scarcely live without them. As Samuel Johnson said in his *Idler,* published originally in a newspaper: ''To us, who are regaled every morning and evening with intelligence, and are supplied from day to day with materials for conversation, it is difficult to conceive how man can subsist without a News-paper, or to what entertainment companies can assemble, in those wide regions of the earth that have neither *Chronicles* nor *Magazines,* neither *Gazettes* nor *Advertisers,* neither *Journals* nor *Evening-Posts.*'' [7] The *Public Advertiser,* which Junius used partly because of its large circulation, usually printed about 3,000 copies a day. The office ledger, now in the British Library, reveals that Junius was good for business, which was of course why Woodfall was willing to run the risk of publishing him. Before the advent of Junius, the paper sold about 2,800 or 2,900 copies a day. When Junius' letters began to appear, circulation rose to an average of about 3,400 copies, and three times exceeded 4,100. The largest-selling issue was that of December 19, 1769 (4,800), when Junius' most famous letter — the "Address to the King" — appeared.

The number of copies, however, does not indicate the number of readers. The coffeehouses received papers, which were handed around and sometimes read aloud. Philip Francis' widow later wrote that "old people have told me that we have no idea of the sensation Junius created at the time in remote little towns. The postman would call out, as he rode through the streets, 'A letter from Junius today!' and all who took in the [*Public Advertiser*] were besieged with requests."[8] A Junius letter which appeared in a morning *Public Advertiser* became, in effect, public property and was always reprinted in later newspapers. When Junius' popularity was established, publishers also began printing pirated collections. The first of these, containing the first fourteen Junius letters, was published by Francis Newbery, who was followed by John Almon and others. Junius, upset by the inaccuracies of these editions, let his own publisher Woodfall know that an authorized collected edition would please him. The hint was taken up, and the authorized edition was published under Junius' scrutiny in March, 1772, two months after Junius' last letter.

By Junius' time the newspaper had clearly proved itself to be a valuable literary medium — and not only for political writers. Johnson's *Idler* papers, unlike the earlier *Rambler,* appeared each Saturday in the *Universal Chronicle,* and Goldsmith's *Citizen of the World* essays originally appeared in *The Public Ledger.* Yet in politics the medium was not entirely respectable. Certainly, Junius' special brand of recurring, scurrilous invective was particularly well-suited to anonymous newspaper publication. The scurrility and repeated attacks could not satisfy the demands of a long pamphlet, nor could the author have survived without anonymity. A newspaper writer need not concern himself with the sustained style, developed arguments, and supporting evidence expected in a pamphlet. In fact, most of the political letters of the time are decidedly third-rate; Junius' letters were dazzlingly superior to his competitors', which largely accounts for his success and power.

But success at invective is not universally admired. Alexander Wedderburn, believed by some to be the author of the Junius letters, hastened to assure the House of Lords that "I have never contaminated my hands with any connexion with a newspaper."[9]

And, more important, the Junius letters were aimed not only at influencing, and perhaps intimidating, members of Parliament, but also at arousing the "mob," which was a formidable force in eighteenth-century politics, as the career of Wilkes admirably demonstrates. Many must have shared the sentiment of Mrs. Montague, that "it was better in old times, when the Ministry was wicked and the mob foolish. Ministers, however wicked, do not pull down houses, nor ignorant mobs pull down Governments. A mob that can read, and a Ministry that cannot think, are sadly matched."[10] In a word, the relatively new medium of newspaper writing offered enough power to inspire fear.

III   Who Was Junius?

The question of identity has been raised distressingly often, especially during the nineteenth century. Disraeli was compelled to give this advice: "Never in society ask who wrote Junius' letters, or if you do, you will be voted a bore." The larger question, Who was Junius? cannot be answered by a simple name, no matter how authoritatively offered, for Junius was not simply an anonymous writer. He was that; but he was also a powerful political force, an important part of the history of a fascinating time, and a talented author and rhetorician. The real answer must come from multiple points of view — some literary, some historical, most, finally, a combination. These points of view will be explored in the rest of this book. For the moment, the following answers may suggest the diversity of the "real" Junius.

To King George III, Junius was an unknown political writer with altogether too large a readership; a man of dangerous political beliefs, who opposed the king on almost every important political measure and who held dangerously false beliefs about the evil influence of the crown and the desirability of more active power by the Parliament and populace; a man of despicable impudence, who attacked and insulted not only the king's ministers but also the king himself.

To the king's ministers, he was the leading and most dangerous of the antiministerial writers, who therefore had to be countered by proministerial writers, however incapable they were of approaching the effectiveness of their antagonist. He was a man with an uncanny sense of detecting the most private concerns of the ministers, displaying them to the public, and interpreting them, without charity, in the most embarrassing, damning, and unfair way possible. He was a man who opposed their political actions at every step, arousing parliamentary and public resentment, and who was apparently determined to destroy every minister until the king acquiesced to Grenville or Chatham. And, he was a man to be discovered and silenced.

To thoughtful political writers of the time, like Johnson or Burke, he was a political writer whose works, by virtue of their cutting style, invective, and ideas, demanded to be read. At the same time he was, to Johnson, a man of despicable politics and, to Burke, a man of inexcusable irreverence.

To a political philosopher, Junius was a phenomenon of the eighteenth century who, adopting the modern idiom of Locke, engaged in numerous skirmishes in the cause of freedom, combining political principles readily available to a Whig constitutionalist of his age, but not thinking about them with the originality or depth of Burke.

To a rhetorician, Junius was a fascinating and talented manipulator of public opinion, a sophisticated, educated, and passionate man who knew the tools of his trade and wielded them expertly.

To a literary historian, Junius was the leading newspaper satirist in an age of satire. His venomous invective was a minor branch of the tradition of satire, but within the limited literary form that he chose to write, Junius' letters are the finest achievement.

To a biographer, Junius has been — a mystery. For over a century the object of numerous theories of identification, he is now, on the basis of considerable evidence, generally recognized to be Philip Francis, a War Office clerk who later became an important councillor in India and a member of Parliament.

CHAPTER 2

The Identity of Junius

ONE of the best-kept secrets in the history of English literature has been the authorship of the Junius letters. "I am the sole depositary of my own secret, and it shall perish with me," Junius wrote in the "Dedication" and the words have proved to be very nearly prophetic.[1] Next to the excellence of the letters themselves, the secrecy of their authorship seems to have been Junius' special care. Junius was, as his epigraph proclaimed, *nominis umbra* — the shadow of a name.[2]

The most certain way for contemporaries to detect Junius would have been through his publisher, Henry Sampson Woodfall. There had to be links between the two for Junius to get his public and private letters to Woodfall and for Woodfall to get private letters, information, and printed copy back to Junius. Therefore, Junius took elaborate precautions to prevent detection. The crucial element, however, was the honesty of Woodfall. If Woodfall's curiosity had overpowered him — and this must have been a tempting possibility, given the mystery surrounding the letters — he probably could have discovered the identity of Junius. But avarice alone might have recalled the story of the goose that laid the golden eggs. By all reports, however, Woodfall was simply an honest, trustworthy businessman; Junius' confidence was well placed. With this confidence between publisher and author, which was the *sine qua non* for the enterprise, Junius sent his letters directly to Woodfall, probably by a messenger unaware of the fame of his employer. On one occasion, however, a tall man in a light overcoat threw a Junius letter in the door of the publisher, then disappeared in a carriage, leaving one person in the office with the impression that the tall man must have been the real Junius. When Woodfall had a parcel to send to his anonymous correspondent, Junius insisted on more indirection. First, Woodfall would plant a signal in the *Public Advertiser* — often "C.," though Junius feared too much repetition even of this: "Don't always use the same signal. — any absurd

22

Latin verse will answer the purpose" (p. 378). Woodfall then sent the parcel to a coffeehouse, the particular place being changed often to avoid detection: "Change to the *Somerset Coffeehouse, &* let no mortal know the alteration. I am persuaded you are too honest a man to contribute in any way to my destruction. Act honorably by me, & at a proper time you shall know me" (p. 376).

Part of Junius' insistence on secrecy must have been based on prudent fear; if he were discovered, after having attacked the king and slandered numerous ministers, he would be subject to criminal action or worse. His first victim, Sir William Draper, was eager to duel his anonymous attacker, if he could only discover him. "It is by no means necessary," Junius coolly observed to him, "that I should be exposed to the resentment of the worst and the most powerful men in this country, though I may be indifferent about yours. Though *you* would fight, there are others who would assassinate" (p. 129). On another occasion he wrote privately to Woodfall: "I must be more cautious than ever. I am sure I should not survive a Discovery three days or if I did, they would attaint me by bill" (p. 376).

The fear of being detected was only part of Junius' motives for secrecy, however. His effectiveness as a powerful writer stemmed directly from his anonymity. No one could read the brilliant invective without wondering who had created it, and it seemed all the more wonderful for its continued obscurity. During Junius' time, and until the middle of the next century, devotees passionately pursued the mystery, hoping to find some key to enter the inner sanctum of the shadowy author, yet the mystery persisted. It took nearly two centuries before the mystery was solved beyond doubt — or, some would say, almost beyond doubt. Much circumstantial evidence exists, but clear, unequivocal facts have long eluded the pursuers.

The quest for the historical Junius, as it has rather grandly been called, is one of guesses, hypotheses, counterhypotheses, brazen assumptions, cool scrutiny, fanciful creation, and even computer analysis. The substance of the hypotheses is varied and fascinating: the tall man in a light coat, feigned handwriting, a vellum set of the *Letters,* a messenger, a love poem, a widow's garbled testimony, noblemen's and publishers' anecdotes, manuscripts, watermarks, illegal reports of parliamentary speeches, biographical data, and, of course, the public and private letters of Junius himself.

I *The Candidates*

For over a century a great deal of printer's ink was spilled over the question, Who was Junius? and one "definitive" solution followed another. A small sampling of titles may suggest the rampant contradictions of the debate: *Junius Discovered* [to be John Horne Tooke] (1789), *The Miscellaneous Works of Hugh Boyd, the Author of the Letters of Junius* (1800), *Reasons for Rejecting the Presumptive Evidence . . . that Mr. Hugh Boyd Was the Writer of Junius, with Passages Selected to Prove the Real Author* [General Charles Lee] (1807), *Letters . . . Proving a Late Prime Minister* [the duke of Portland] *to Have Been Junius* (1816), *Junius Unmasked* [as Edward Gibbon] (1819), *Junius Unmasked; or Lord George Sackville Proved to be Junius* (1828), *Junius Lord Chatham* (1838), *Junius Discovered* (1854), *Junius Finally Revealed* (1917), etc. Book after book was published on the mystery, plus scores of journal articles advancing claims equally confident and diverse. There have been at least fifty different names put forward in print as the real Junius. Among them are some of the most prominent men of the day: Edmund Burke, Lord Chatham, Lord Chesterfield, Edward Gibbon, George Grenville, John Wilkes, Horace Walpole, and Thomas Paine.

Among the earliest candidates, according to Horace Walpole, "three were especially suspected, Wilkes, Edmund Burke, and William Gerard Hamilton.... Hamilton was most generally suspected."[3] "Single-speech Hamilton," as he was dubbed on the basis of his one speaking appearance in Parliament, denied the authorship of the letters, though he claimed he could have written them better. The only reason he was suspected of the authorship appears to be that on one occasion he reported to the duke of Richmond the substance of a Junius letter he claimed to have read in the *Public Advertiser*. The letter, however, was not there; instead there was an apology for a delay, and the letter that Hamilton spoke of was printed the following day. This could conceivably be evidence of authorship, but there were problems: Hamilton's politics were quite unlike Junius' on some matters, such as parliamentary reform, and furthermore he was not in England when some of the letters were published. If the anecdote about Hamilton's knowledge is true, it is more likely that Woodfall read the letter to him than that he wrote it.

The quality of letters led many to ascribe them to the greatest political writer of his day, Edmund Burke. So astute a judge as Samuel Johnson, who knew Burke well, said in 1775 that "he looked upon Burke to be the author of Junius, and though he would not take him *contra mundum,* yet he would take him against any man." However, Johnson was later convinced by the sincerity of Burke's denial. Boswell reported a conversation on the subject: "Talking of the wonderful concealment of the authour of the celebrated letters signed *Junius*; he [Johnson] said, 'I should have believed Burke to be Junius, because I know no man but Burke who is capable of writing these letters; but Burke spontaneously denied it to me. The case would have been different had I asked him if he was the authour; a man so questioned, as to an anonymous publication, may think he has a right to deny it.' "[4] Johnson was not alone in suspecting Burke to be Junius. Many newspaper writers accused Burke of being the author, and Sir William Draper, the unfortunate victim of the early letters who wanted to duel his anonymous antagonist, purposely sought a confession or denial from Burke and had to be content with the latter.

A prominent London bookseller named John Almon, who published a considerable amount of political writing during the time of Junius and was privy to all the political gossip, caught a glimpse of Junius' handwriting from Woodfall's manuscript and immediately associated it with the hand of Hugh Macauley Boyd, a young Irishman who often frequented his bookstore. When he next met Boyd, Almon said to him, "I have seen part of one of Junius' letters, in manuscript, which I believe is your handwriting," to which Boyd changed color and responded only that this did not constitute conclusive proof. On this basis and very little more, Almon and others concluded that Boyd was indeed Junius. Boyd was in fact an enthusiastic admirer of Junius' politics and even imitated him in his own writings, which strengthened his claim, though his writings were far inferior to Junius'. Some people were genuinely flattered to be suspected as Junius, and therefore encouraged the suspicion. This appears to be the case with Boyd. Neither Almon nor anyone else had the least proof that he was Junius; it was a mere guess, but not an unbelievable one.

II   *More Junius, Public and Private*

Interest in Junius by no means died when Junius disappeared in 1772. The collected edition of his letters published by Woodfall, complete with a preface, a long "Dedication to the English Nation," and notes by Junius himself, insured Junius' prolonged existence. In addition, there were many pirated editions of the letters, posing as "authorized editions," and numerous reprints. A particularly fine edition, "with Notes and Illustrations, Historical, Political, Biographical, and Critical," by Robert Heron, appeared in 1802. Heron's edition was a far cry from the usual reprint. It included a lengthy essay on the eloquence, political principles, and authorship of Junius (Heron's candidate was Dunning, Lord Ashburton), and preceding each letter, elaborate rhetorical and political "observations," plus lengthy notes on Junius' text, all done by an accomplished mind in a graceful style.

The most important later edition of Junius, however, appeared in 1812, published by George Woodfall, the son of the original publisher, H. S. Woodfall. The publisher and his editor, J. Mason Good, had access to all of Junius' publications in the *Public Advertiser,* and, more important, to Junius' private correspondence with John Wilkes and with H. S. Woodfall. These were all incorporated into the new edition, constituting a sizable new body of Junian material. The sixty-three letters from Junius to his publisher were of special interest to those who sought to know the real Junius. The letters do not reveal the secret — Woodfall remained completely in the dark about his mysterious correspondent — but they do give a glimpse of the nonpublic Junius, writing off the record. The private letters sometimes deal with the publishing of the Junius letters or transmitting information, with plans for the collected edition, and occasionally with personal information ("I have been out of town these three weeks" [p. 356]). But the letters also reveal Junius making pungent comments about politics and political writers ("This Scaevola is the wretchedest of all fools; & a dirty knave" [p. 382]) which correspond to the fiery temperament of the published letters.

The bulk of Mason Good's three-volume edition consisted of a long "Preliminary Essay on Junius and His Writings" and an astonishing collection of some one hundred "miscellaneous letters" with various signatures — "Popicola," "Corregio," "Mnemon," "C.," "Atticus," "Veteran," etc. — which Mason Good said were written by Junius. Good's authority for these new attributions came in a general way from the hitherto unknown private letters. "I sometimes change my Signature," Junius had written to Woodfall, "but could have no reason to change the paper, especially for one that does not circulate half so much as Yours" (p. 358). Junius' private comments do make clear that he was responsible for some letters not in the collected edition; a gross reply to "Junia," for example, which Junius decided was "idle and improper," was clearly his, as were the "Veteran" attacks on Lord Barrington.

However, this accounts for very few of the hundred letters which Good added to the canon of sixty known Junius letters, and Good offered almost no justification for attributing the rest to Junius. Having access to Woodfall's files, Good might have had some secret information about Junius' authorship of them, but none was forthcoming. In truth, Good seems to have attributed them to Junius on the basis of style alone. It was not until 1848 — thirty-six years later — that anyone challenged the validity of Good's attributions.

In that year Charles Wentworth Dilke, editor of the prestigious journal *Athenaeum,* began a series of articles on Junius. Several of his early articles were devoted to examining Good's edition, which he found to be unsound in a number of ways. Dilke was himself an excellent scholar, well versed in Junian matters; under his scrutiny, Good's methods were exposed as shoddy and careless. Dilke argued very convincingly that "what Good calls *proof* is mere speculative opinion"; in short, most of Good's attributions were based on Good's thinking their style to be like Junius'. This was not at all clear from Good's confident, assertive essay; the attributions had appeared as unquestionable facts, not opinions. Dilke suspected that the real reason for the abundant "miscellaneous letters" was that the publisher wanted to fill up three volumes. He also scrutinized Good's "Preliminary Essay" and pronounced it to be "a piece of pure imaginative writing."[5] Still more damning, Dilke pointed out that the dates prefixed to the private letters, as if they were part of the letters, were not Junius' dates at all: they were Good's, and furthermore some were patently wrong.

However, until the advent of Dilke on the Junian scene, no one questioned the authority of what was called "Woodfall's Junius" (since Good's editing had been done anonymously). On the problem of authorship, however, Mason Good provided considerably more evidence to work from — some genuine, some spurious — and cleared the field of the most prominent contenders, but offered no leads of his own.

III *The Case for Philip Francis*

It was not long before readers of Mason Good's edition began using his evidence in support of new candidates. In 1813, John Taylor, best known to literary students as Keats' publisher, brought forth a hypothesis based directly on the new "miscellaneous" letters of Junius. Following clues in the Veteran letters and in Junius' emphatic insistence on Woodfall's secrecy, Taylor concluded that Junius was two people: Reverend Francis, the translator of Horace, and his son Philip, who worked as chief clerk in the War Office for "that bloody wretch Barrington." On further investigation, however, Taylor decided that Philip Francis was the sole author of the Junius letters; this thesis appeared in his second book, *The Identity of Junius with a Distinguished Living Character Established* (1816).

The case Taylor built in this book and its supplement the following year was formidable and influential, though he had no confession or undeniable proof for his argument. Rather it was a series of striking coincidences and an accumulation of circumstantial evidence that he rested his case on. Francis, though a young man at the time of the Junius letters, had had considerable experience in politics. In 1756 he was given a junior clerkship in the secretary of state's office, which began a series of political connections: he became secretary to General Bligh, then secretary to Lord Kinnoul, who was the ambassador to Lisbon, and Latin secretary to Chatham. In 1763 he was appointed to a responsible position in the War Office, a position he held throughout the existence of Junius. Junius appeared to Taylor to be closely allied to the War Office because of his extensive knowledge of military matters: the dismissal of Sir Jeffrey Amherst, the rescue of General Gansell, the preferment of General Burgoyne, the terms of Sir William Draper's regiment, the conduct of Lord Granby, and, above all, the new appointments in the War Office which prompted his malicious attack on Lord Barrington. Francis was in a position to know the details of all of these cases.

The dates of Francis' residence in London and his travels correspond closely to the appearance of the letters. When Francis was out of London, Junius was silent. For example, in Letter LVI Horne mocked Junius for not replying to Horne's letter of July 31, 1771, until August 13. Horne used the silence to taunt his adversary: "I congratulate you, Sir, on the recovery of your wonted style, though it has cost you a fortnight. I compassionate your labour in the composition of your letters" (I, 396). If Junius were Francis, the two-week silence was not devoted to the labor of composition; Francis had left London at the end of July and returned on August 11 or 12.

The cessation of the letters in 1772 also corresponds to a break in Francis' life. The last Junius letter appeared in the *Public Advertiser* on January 21. On the same day, Francis' close friend and superior in the War Office, D'Oyly, resigned, and Barrington appointed Chamier as the new deputy secretary. Junius reported this to Woodfall on January 24, announcing his intention to torture the "bloody wretch" Barrington under the alias "Veteran." It is this series, running from January 28 to May 12, which glorifies D'Oyly and Francis at the expense of Barrington and Chamier. Woodfall heard from Junius on May 10, 1772, but then came a long silence. Francis had left his position in the War Office in March and in July left England for a tour of the Continent. He returned on December 14, 1772, had to go immediately to Bath to visit his ill father, and returned to London on January 12 or 13, 1773. One week later, after a silence of six months, Junius wrote a farewell letter to Woodfall, clearly indicating that Junius would write no more. In May Francis traveled to The Hague, then he was appointed to the governing council of India, where he departed on March, 1774. If Junius and Francis were one and the same, the coincidences in these dates would be easily explained. And an early memoir of Francis which appeared in the *Monthly Mirror* of 1810 stated that Francis had left the War Office "in consequence of a difference with Viscount Barrington, by whom he thought himself injured."[6] This would apparently explain the vicious attacks by Junius on Barrington, though this was later complicated by the discovery that Francis and Barrington parted on amicable terms and that Barrington himself obtained the India post for Francis.[7]

Junius might have attacked Lord Holland in his letters since, as an ally of Bute, he differed greatly in his politics from Junius, but he did not; in fact, in a private letter to Woodfall, he even expressed some partiality for him: "I wish Lord Holland may acquit himself with honour" (p. 351). There was good reason for Francis to practice this forbearance. His father was Lord Holland's domestic chaplain and tutor to his son, dedicated his translation of Demosthenes to Lord Holland as his patron, and owed all of his church preferments to Holland's influence. Hence there was considerable family debt to Holland. And Philip Francis himself was given his first political job, the clerkship in the secretary of state's office, by Lord Holland. The private letters also reveal a particular regard for the publisher Woodfall, which could be explained by the fact that Francis and Woodfall were schoolmates at St. Paul's; they knew each other there and were friendly, though not close, in later life.

It appears from the letters that Junius was not a member of Parliament, though he often attended as an auditor and made notes on the debates. During the debate over the Falkland Islands Junius seems to have been worried about admission to Parliament. "It is of the utmost importance to the Public Cause that the Doors of the House of Lords should be opened on Tuesday next," he wrote to Woodfall, and included two announcements for Woodfall to print in order to "shame" them into admitting the public (p. 367). This suggests that he could not otherwise hear the debate, yet if he were an M.P. he would have privileged entree into both Houses. Francis did not become a member of Parliament until 1783, but he often attended as a spectator and even reported several speeches by Chatham which Junius also reported.

Junius and Francis were in remarkable accord in their political beliefs. Though generally Whiggish, neither was committed to any party line, but maintained an independence of thought which led them to differ from all others. When Francis opposed a reform bill in 1784, he said, "I am not a party man on this or any other question."[8] Junius likewise considered himself to be "disowned, as a dangerous auxiliary, by every party in the kingdom" (p. 228). Yet they did not differ from each other. Both greatly admired, though with qualification, Lord Chatham — "a great, illustrious, faulty, human being," Francis called him[9] — and both approved of the policies of George Grenville. They also took the same stand on particular issues — supporting the right to tax colonies though questioning the wisdom of it, supporting triennial though abhorring annual and septennial Parliaments, and opposing the extension of the elective franchise to large trading towns. Junius did not favor the abolition of rotten boroughs and Francis in Parliament did, but Francis confessed that he had once thought otherwise.

Some contemporaries suspected that Junius was an Irishman, the most palpable piece of evidence being his use of the word "collegian," which was of common usage in Ireland but not in England. In fact, Francis was Irish, though he had moved to London at age ten. Taylor also found that both Francis and Junius used some unusual phrases which suggested common authorship — phrases like "a false fact," "of our side" rather than "on our side," "so far forth," and "examinable," and an odd use of the verb "mean," as in "I meant the Cause & the public" (p. 393). Taylor could also point to some similarities in the handwriting of Junius and Francis.

Taylor had done an impressive piece of sleuthing. Beginning with a hunch based on the Veteran letters of Mason Good's edition, and after a semifalse start, which led him to the father instead of the son, he built up one piece of evidence after another, some internal, based on the letters themselves, and some external, based on what he knew about Philip Francis. The case was essentially complete. It has been scrutinized, summarized, attacked, and bolstered since 1816, but the pro-Francis argument we now know is essentially what Taylor put forward over a century and a half ago. No single fact was sufficient to prove that Francis was Junius, but the collection and combination of circumstantial evidence that Taylor presented made a powerful case. Chief Justice Dallas, who presided over a number of trials, said he would have cheerfully hanged Francis on the evidence presented by Taylor — presuming it to have been a hanging matter. But there was still the possibility that new evidence would appear, perhaps some one undeniable fact to add to Taylor's argument. After all, Francis was still alive when Taylor published his *Junius Identified* and presumably had personal reasons for not acknowledging the authorship. New evidence, like the much-sought vellum-bound letters which Woodfall sent to Junius, might appear in the future.

More Junius material did appear, though not the vellum set and not any single decisive fact. In 1840 the editors of the *Chatham Correspondence* published two letters from Junius to Chatham, and in 1853 three more Junius letters appeared, this time in the *Grenville Papers,* but the mystery of identity remained. More intriguing revelations came from Lady Francis, Sir Philip's widow, in 1847. In a long and fascinating letter published in Lord Campbell's *Lives of the Lord Chancellors,* Lady Francis discussed what "I can have no doubts on" — namely, that her husband was Junius. It was a curious arrangement: Sir Philip never confessed the authorship to his second wife, yet in many ways he encouraged her to believe it. "Though his manner and conversation on that mysterious subject were such as to leave me not a shadow of doubt on the fact of his being the author, telling me circumstances that none but Junius could know," she wrote, "he never avowed himself more than saying he knew what my opinion was, and never contradicting it." His first gift to his wife was an edition of Junius. She was instructed to take it to her room and never let it be seen, nor ever speak of it. On his death, Francis left a sealed package directed to his wife: a copy of Taylor's *Junius Identified,* the book which argued that Francis was Junius.[10]

Lady Francis' narrative bears some likeness to a much less sympathetic hypothesis put forward anonymously by DeQuincey many years earlier in the *Edinburgh Evening Post* of 1827 and 1828. DeQuincey accepted Taylor's arguments completely, but felt that Taylor had missed the significance of Francis' secrecy. The real key, said DeQuincey, was "GUILT: the consciousness that, by claiming his literary honours, he should cover himself with infamy as a man. This, and nothing *but* this, can be the cause that Junius has not long ago — either by himself or by his representatives — come forward to claim his rights."[11] First, according to this theory, Francis betrayed the secrets of the War Office and was thus "a traitor to his duties"; because of their secret information, the Junius letters were "one long act of systematic perfidy." But even worse was a second betrayal — a betrayal of the English people, to whom he had dedicated his author's edition. Having lost his position in the War Office, DeQuincey argued, Junius' source of information no longer existed. Therefore, Francis withdrew to the Continent and secretly negotiated with the government: for a price, Junius would write no more. Shortly, Francis had a seat on the Council of Bengal and Junius was dead. The terms were absolute secrecy on both sides, freedom from Junius' malice for the government, and a lucrative appointment for Francis. DeQuincey's evidence was twofold: Francis' salary jumped from 400 pounds per year as a clerk in the War Office to 10,000 pounds per year for the India appointment — a discrepancy otherwise defying explanation — and a story related in Sir Nathaniel Wraxall's *Memoirs.* The king reportedly rode out with General Desaguliers in 1772 and said in conversation, "We know who Junius is, and he will write no more." Thus, having betrayed the ministry by revealing their secrets, Francis then betrayed the people by silencing Junius for a sizeable sum of hush-money.

Other modifications appeared as time passed: John Wade, in his two-volume Bohn edition of Junius published in 1850, proposed a more honorable account than DeQuincey's; Francis' grandson was more inclined to the hush-money theory;[12] and Joseph Parkes and Herman Merivale published Francis' *Memoirs,* which contained much interesting new material but no direct evidence for the identification. Charles Chabot pursued Taylor's leads about Junius' handwriting, finding additional evidence, and Leslie Stephen rigorously examined the relations between Junius, Francis, and Chatham to the advancement of the Franciscan theory.[13]

IV *Unbelievers and Alternatives*

The argument for Philip Francis received considerable support from impressive judges — not only DeQuincey but also Lord Brougham, Lord Campbell, Macaulay, and Lecky, to mention a few. But the lack of hard, clear evidence — the "one *fact*" on which purists like Dilke and W. Fraser Rae insisted — haunted the cause and, despite all the circumstantial evidence, the claim seemed to keep slipping away from Francis after periods of apparent conviction. In the "Introductory Epistle" to *The Fortunes of Nigel* (1822), Sir Walter Scott discussed the benefits of an incognito: "But a cause, however ingeniously pleaded, is not therefore gained. You may remember, the neatly-wrought chain of circumstantial evidence, so artificially brought forward to prove Sir Philip Francis's title to the Letters of Junius, seemed at first irrefragable; yet the influence of the reasoning has passed away, and Junius, in the general opinion, is as much unknown as ever."

The claims for Francis, then, were by no means universally admitted after Taylor's identification and certainly not after the scrutiny of Dilke. There were many other candidates put forward in the nineteenth century. The claims ranged from the ridiculous to the plausible and were put forward by people ranging from cranks, who had no ability at research and no scruples about ignoring obvious contradictory evidence, to professional librarians and men of letters, who brought solid learning and talent to the pursuit of Junius. One of the former — and we will do no more than cast one brief glance at this unfortunately large group — was William Cramp, who discovered what, according to him, the duke of Grafton and other high government officials had definitely known in 1770 — that Lord Chesterfield was Junius. The marvel of this discovery is that Lord Chesterfield was seventy-five years old when the first Junius letter was published; he had ended his political career fifteen years earlier when he gave his last speech in Parliament (the speech fatigued him so much that he had to be carried home), and had steadily declined in health from that day. When the Junius letters appeared, Chesterfield was paralyzed in his lower limbs and had lost much of the use of his upper limbs, he had been completely deaf for twelve years, and had poor eyesight, so poor that he was blind for months on end. The one point in Cramp's favor was that Lord Chesterfield was indeed alive when the Junius letters were published. But he was tottering on his grave and finally died in the month of Junius' last letter, which was Cramp's "clue" to the authorship of the most vigorous prose of the age. To this discovery Cramp devoted no less than two eminently forgettable books and four pamphlets.[14]

Many other candidates were brought forward, some relatively plausible, by more competent intellects. John Britton revived the eighteenth-century notion that the letters were written by Colonel Isaac Barré and undertook the "arduous and delicate task" of proving it.[15] And the editor of the *Grenville Papers,* W. J. Smith, contributed not only new Junius letters — which Junius had written to George Grenville — but also an entirely new candidate. For many years it had been rumored that the Grenvilles owned important and as yet unknown Junius letters. In 1828 the *Morning Post* announced to its readers that "five letters are deposited in the archives of the GRENVILLE family at Stow, which are said to establish, beyond the possibility of doubt, the real author of Junius."[16] The owner, however, refused to allow them to be published. When Smith published the three (not five) letters in 1853, they failed to live up to the rumors. Smith prefaced the fourth volume of the papers with a long, 216-page essay trying to prove that Junius was George Grenville's older brother, Lord Temple. But far from proving it "beyond the possibility of doubt," Smith himself was not even convinced, as he confessed at the end of his essay.[17] However, less scrupulous men than Smith, including some advocates of Philip Francis, were often convinced by far less evidence.

V *Twentieth-Century Views*

By the beginning of the twentieth century Francis was firmly established as the leading candidate. Junius was either Francis or some unknown person, but most likely he was Francis. The biographies of Parkes and Merivale and of Leslie Stephen seriously weakened the influence of Dilke's skepticism, though since no final proof had been produced, the skepticism was by no means ended. Everything in favor of Francis seemed to have been said; thus, what was written on Junius tended to be skeptical or in support of other candidates. Because of this, when one examines twentieth-century Junius studies, he may get the misleading impression that the case for Francis was weakening.

In the early part of the century, confident "discoveries" were still being made. In 1909 an author named James Smith revealed that the real author of the letters was Edward Gibbon, who, Smith gloated, was in his own time "never so much as suspected!"[18] Smith ingenuously confessed that "on a careful scrutiny of each link in the chain of evidence which I have welded together, I have been unable to discover any trace of weakness," and for this reason he did not feel compelled to make the least allusion to the claims of Francis. The chain, however, was not as artfully welded as Smith believed. It consisted of observations that Junius' "Address to the King" had, without doubt, a "true Gibbonian ring," that Junius was a good classicist and Gibbon a preeminent classical scholar, and so forth. A few years later, a title page shouted "EUREKA": Junius was finally discovered, to the author's satisfaction, to be Thomas Paine.[19]

Naturally, these discoveries took place at the outer fringes of the literary and scholarly world, unlike those of the nineteenth century, which were debated by eminent men of letters in leading journals like the *Athenaeum*. But in 1927 a well-known historian, C. W. Everett, published a new edition of Junius in which he argued for Lord Shelburne's authorship. Shelburne was not a new candidate (nor indeed was Gibbon or Paine) and Everett had very little new to say for his authorship; in fact, he did not even counter Dilke's objections to the earlier claims. The edition was reviewed by a still more famous historian, Lewis B. Namier, but this did not signal a return of Junius studies to its former glory. On the contrary, Namier's review was titled "Where Scholars Tread no More" and contained nothing but scorn for Everett's argument. "The one thing more idle than propounding a theory on flimsy grounds," he asserted, "would be to waste time on disproving it by elaborate research."[20] The question of the authorship of Junius' letters, once an urgent issue to contemporaries, then fascinating, then at least interesting, seemed to be dying an ignominious death, partly through neglect and, when not neglect, through repetitive, dull attention.

But before the burial — or uninterred decay — of the authorship question, one more book appeared on the subject, appropriately titled *Who Was Junius?* (1962). Far from bringing the subject to an ignominious end, the book by Alvar Ellegard proved to be one of the most sensible and interesting works written about Junius since the beginning of the debate. Ellegard began his search thinking that Junius was probably *not* Francis. To find out who was, he decided to pursue the lead of Junius' handwriting. He examined the subscription registers and matriculation lists at English universities and law schools, thousands of eighteenth-century wills, and manuscripts housed in the British Museum and Bodleian Library, but found nothing resembling Junius' hand.

He then turned to a statistical analysis of Junius' style. There had of course been numerous arguments that Junius' style resembled not only that of Francis but scores of others, and it was precisely this indiscriminate application of the argument that rendered it useless as proof. Ellegard, however, was going to rely not on impressions but on statistics, aided by that distinctive twentieth-century device, the computer. He devised an ingenious and original method for putting the computer to work on the authorship problem.

In order to know the peculiarities of Junius' writings, Ellegard had to measure them against other contemporary writings. He therefore assembled a "million word sample" of non-Junius writing to compare with the 82,200 words in the 1772 edition of Junius. Then he compiled an extensive testing list of words and phrases that Junius used more often than his contemporaries (called "Junius plus-expressions") and words and phrases that he used markedly less often than his contemporaries ("Junius minus-expressions"). The computer could mathematically determine precisely how distinctive each expression was. To compensate for the relative infrequency of each of the 272 expressions on the testing list, Ellegard devised a technique called "grouping." Expressions with similar distinctiveness were put together into eighteen groups — nine for plus-expressions and nine for minus-expressions. When these were measured against Francis' usage and the usage of fifty-nine other contemporary political writers, it appeared to a striking degree that in all groups, as Ellegard says, "the words avoided by Junius are avoided by Francis, the words favoured by Junius are favoured by Francis."[21]

This test in itself established a very high probability that Junius was Francis — and made a Franciscan of Ellegard — but he ran another test on completely separate linguistic data, which raised the probability even higher. There are many roughly synonymous alternatives in the English language — like "hardly" and "scarcely," "commonly" and "usually," "until" and "till" — and any writer has habitual preferences. Taking considerable pains to establish an unbiased list of such alternatives, Ellegard arrived at the same conclusion: Philip Francis again attained the highest score. A few exceptions proved the rule. For example, Junius consistently preferred "upon" to "on," but Francis preferred the latter. On a closer look, however, Ellegard discovered Francis' usage on this word underwent a rapid change when he went to India. During the Junius years, Francis' use of "upon" was similar to Junius'. Likewise, in his early writings Francis preferred "until" to "till" — which squares with Junius' usage — though later in his life he more often used "till." It was not just impressions, then, but statistics which supported Ellegard's conclusion: "Not only is Francis' language, considered as a whole, more like that of Junius than that of any other contemporary writer examined: those Francis texts whose subject-matter and general character are nearest to Junius are indistinguishable from the authenticated Junius letters."[22]

Of course, it must be recognized that Ellegard has not proved absolutely that Junius was Francis; he has — to be technically accurate — simply established an extremely high probability on linguistic evidence alone that Junius was Francis. This, however, coupled with other Francis evidence and with the weak claims of other candidates, puts the case on firm ground. What Taylor discovered in 1813, what Merivale, Stephen, and Chabot confirmed with further facts and analysis in the later nineteenth century, and what Ellegard has more recently confirmed by a computerized stylistic analysis, seems as near fact as human beings may reasonably expect to come: Junius, we may safely say, was Philip Francis.[23]

The mystery of Junius' identity proved fascinating to many people, especially in the last century, but it also had an unfortunate side effect: the question of authorship so completely dominated discussions of Junius that his real merit as a literary and historical phenomenon went virtually ignored.

CHAPTER 3

Wilkes and Liberty

T HE political career of John Wilkes is one of the most fascinating in the eighteenth century. Bon vivant, rake, member of the notorious Hell Fire Club, author of an obscene poem, he was expelled from Parliament, reelected then rejected by the House of Commons three times, imprisoned in the Tower, outlawed, and convicted of libel and blasphemy. Yet Wilkes was the favorite of the London mob, a skillful political propagandist, and a politician of great importance in establishing English liberties. Whether we choose it or not, as Gladstone observed, the name of Wilkes must be enrolled among the great champions of English freedom. As defenders of that shibboleth "liberty," Wilkes and Junius found themselves fighting for a common cause. Because of Wilkes' notoriety and, more important, because of the constitutional crisis which he precipitated, his cause figures more prominently than any other in *The Letters of Junius*.

I *That Devil Wilkes*

Wilkes was called many scurrilous names during his political career, but the most famous epithet — "that devil Wilkes" — was bestowed on him by no less a person than the king of England, George III. The combined qualities of charm, invective, talent, and a quick eye for opportunity gave Wilkes the knack of raising passions in his political opponents, in the London mob, and, though he was singularly ugly, in beautiful women. After having dinner with Wilkes, the historian Edward Gibbon wrote, "I scarcely ever met with a better Companion; he has inexhaustible spirits, infinite wit, and humour, and a great deal of knowledge; but a thorough profligate in principle as in practice; his character is infamous, his life stained with every vice, and his conversation full of blasphemy and bawdy."[1] This charming, corrupt character raised a political

38

turmoil in England during the 1760s and 1770s matched only by the American Revolution. By the time the Junius letters appeared on the scene, Wilkes had established himself as a thorn in the side of the government and a hero of the mob.

Educated in Presbyterian schools and the University of Leyden, Wilkes returned to England at age twenty-two to marry a wealthy woman ten years older than himself. The match produced a daughter to whom Wilkes was devoted and provided enough money to launch his political career, but otherwise was a total failure ending in separation. Much better suited to Wilkes' temperament was the companionship of Sir Francis Dashwood, Lord Sandwich, the poet Charles Churchill, and others who called themselves the Monks of Medmenham Abbey. In this brilliant, dissipated company, assisted by honorary nuns, Wilkes enjoyed the conviviality, debauchery, and Black Masses of the notorious Hell Fire Club. He entered Parliament for Aylesbury in 1757 while a member of the Club and was returned in the general election of 1761, the first election in the reign of George III. When Lord Bute launched the progovernment journal *The Briton* with Smollett as editor, Wilkes countered it by anonymously publishing an opposition journal, *The North Briton.*

The new journal was an immediate success. It soon had more readers than the government journals and contributed to their speedy demise. In the first issue Wilkes announced that *"the liberty of the Press* is the birthright of a Briton" and began to exercise the right zealously with satire, innuendo, and insult directed at government ministers and supporters like Bute, Johnson, Smollett, and Hogarth.

When the Grenville ministry replaced the Bute ministry in April, 1763, Parliament was presented with what is commonly called the king's speech — in fact the speech of the new ministry. On hearing the policies of the Bute ministry defended and even glorified, Wilkes published his famous forty-fifth *North Briton.* The king's name, Wilkes said, had been attached to "odious measures," to the "fallacious and baneful" Peace of Paris, to "gross blunders," "corruptions and despotism," and "wicked instruments of oppression." "I lament to see [the honor of the crown] sunk even to prostitution."[2]

Wilkes was correct in his position that the speech was the composition of the ministers and, as such, subject to criticism, but in the eyes of the court party "Number 45" was a direct attack on the sovereign. The king himself ordered Wilkes to be prosecuted

and for several years took a personal interest in ruining Wilkes.
Lord Halifax, the leading secretary of state, issued a general warrant to seize the authors, printers, and publishers of the *North
Briton* and had forty-nine persons arrested. Wilkes was arrested
and confined in the Tower. The concerted effort of the government, however, turned out to be a series of blunders. They did not
realize the potential power of Wilkes, who played his role as royal
antagonist in grand style. In court he aggrandized his situation
from an individual to a national crisis: "The liberty of all peers and
gentlemen, — and (what touches me more sensibly) that of all the
middling and inferior set of people, who stand most in need of protection, — is, in my case, this day to be finally decided upon; a
question of such importance, as to determine at once whether
English liberty be a reality or a shadow."[3] Wilkes struck the right
chord when he appealed to the "middling and inferior set of
people"; they rallied around him and found in Wilkes an obliging
hero and demagogue.

The ministry's anger and desire to ruin Wilkes were under-
standable, but their tactics were based on serious errors of
judgment. Wilkes rested his defense on three constitutional points
of considerable consequence: first, general warrants — that is, warrants which did not specify names — were illegal; second, search
warrants on a charge of libel were illegal; and third, parliamentary
privilege secured him from arrest. On each point Wilkes won his
case. He was not only freed from imprisonment but was awarded
1000 pounds damages and soon instigated a suit against Lord
Halifax. Glorying in his triumph, Wilkes printed on his own press a
complete edition of the *North Briton* and a few copies of an
obscene parody of Pope's *Essay on Man* entitled *An Essay on
Woman.* When Parliament reconvened, the government had
mustered enough support to renew their attack on Wilkes and they
were aided by Wilkes' imprudent publications. Lord Sandwich, a
notorious profligate himself who had once been Wilkes' fellow
monk in the Medmenham Brotherhood, read the *Essay on Woman*
aloud in the House of Lords to display Wilkes' depravity. The
House of Commons declared "Number 45" libelous and ordered it
to be publicly burned by the hangman. Furthermore, they retro-
actively ruled that parliamentary privilege did not cover libel and
expelled Wilkes from membership in the House. Meanwhile,
Wilkes had been seriously wounded in a duel with a parliamentary
antagonist and had eluded government spies to go into voluntary

exile in France. Since he did not appear in court to be tried for seditious libel and blasphemy, he was outlawed in 1764.

For several years Wilkes traveled in France and Italy. He attempted to obtain a pardon so that he could return to England and, on one occasion when the Rockingham ministry was in power, secretly appeared in London for that purpose, but Rockingham already had enough troubles to contend with and would do no more than raise a stipend and send Wilkes back to France. In March, 1768, however, Wilkes appeared openly in London, begged pardon of the king in a letter, and, not receiving an answer, announced his candidacy for a seat in Parliament. He failed to be elected for the City of London but immediately stood for Middlesex and was elected on March 28. The government, now led by Grafton, reluctantly faced a new challenge: a decidedly unrespectable man, charged with libel and blasphemy, and formally pronounced an outlaw, had been chosen by the electorate to sit in the House of Commons. Thus began a constitutional crisis and popular uprising far more serious than the original turmoil over "Number 45."

II   *The Middlesex Controversy*

Although Junius' attachment to Wilkes was to lead some to suspect that the two were actually the same, Junius' support of Wilkes evolved gradually and was never unqualified. At the outset, in fact, Junius' portrayal of Wilkes was calculated to elicit contempt rather than sympathy. Writing under the signature "C" a week after Wilkes' Middlesex election, Junius summarized the Wilkes affair with a peculiar slant:

A man of a most infamous character in private life is indicted for a libel against the King's person, solemnly tried by his peers according to the laws of the land, and found guilty. To avoid the sentence due to his crime he flies to a foreign country, and, failing to surrender himself to justice, is outlawed. By this outlawry he loses all claim to the protection of those magistrates and of those laws to which, by his evasion, he had refused to be amenable. After some years spent abroad, this man returns to England with as little fear of the laws which he had violated as of respect for the great person [the king] whom he had wantonly and treasonably attacked. Without a single qualification, either moral or political, and under the greatest disability, this man presumes so far upon the protection of the populace as to offer himself a candidate to represent the metropolis of the kingdom. . . . We see a man overwhelmed with debts, a convict and an outlaw, returned to serve in the British parliament as knight of a shire. These, Sir, are the main facts of Mr. Wilkes's case.[4]

This portrait of thorough evil foreshadows later Junius portraits not of Wilkes but of Wilkes' enemies.

Junius' early attitude toward Wilkes is explained by the facts that the constitutional issue had not yet developed and that the Wilkite mob had grown riotous almost to the point of anarchy. Later, Junius wrote in a personal letter to Wilkes, "Depend upon it, the perpetual Union of *Wilkes & Mob* does you no service. . . . I would not make myself cheap, by walking the Streets so much as you do" (p. 426). There was considerable distress among the poor in England in the late 1760s. The harvests had been bad, the winters hard, wages low, and unemployment high. Because strikes were numerous, the streets were filled with idle and discontented workers. Wilkes — the unrespectable, colorful outlaw — especially attracted the London sailors and Spitalfield weavers, about six thousand of whom were active Wilkites during the 1768 election. The mob controlled all the avenues leading to Brentford, where the Middlesex election was held, and assaulted the opponents of Wilkes. According to Benjamin Franklin nearly every house within a fifteen mile radius of London had a "45" scrawled on its door in support of Wilkes or fear of the mob. When Wilkes won the election there was great rejoicing: the king's windows were broken, the entire city was ablaze with lights, and the popular cry of "Wilkes and Liberty!" was heard everywhere. Junius was not exaggerating much when he said that London and the royal family "were left, for two nights together, at the mercy of a licentious, drunken rabble" (Wade, II, 166). Since Wilkes was after all an outlaw, Junius blamed the ministry for allowing him to foment "this detestable scene" with apparent impunity.

On April 20 Wilkes insisted on being arrested and was accordingly imprisoned for a short time until Chief Justice Mansfield thought it prudent to cancel the outlawry on a quibble: the writ had been made out "at the County Court for the County of Middlesex" instead of "at the County Court of Middlesex for the County of Middlesex." The government's actions with the general warrant, search warrant, and outlawry had all proven to be illegal, but Wilkes was still faced with the libel and blasphemy charges for the *North Briton* and *Essay on Woman*. For these he was fined 500 pounds and sentenced to twenty-two months in the King's Bench prison. Wilkes numbered among his friends, however, merchants and noblemen as well as the "rabble," and a group of patriotic citizens combined to see that Wilkes did not suffer during his imprisonment. A large subscription was begun which eventually paid out 20,000 pounds for Wilkes' debts, fines, and expenses. Furthermore, Wilkes was consoled by a steady stream of friends, women, and fine food during his stay in jail.

The scene outside King's Bench prison, however, was less cheerful. On May 10 Parliament reconvened and a large crowd gathered outside the prison in St. George's Fields anticipating Wilkes' possible release. The government, which had no intention of releasing him, had feared a riot and taken the precaution of surrounding the prison with troops. The crowd grew very large, the riot act was read and the soldiers ordered to fire. Six people were killed, among them a perfectly innocent young spectator named Allen. The incident, called the Massacre of St. George's Fields, aroused indignation among the populace and opposition.

The government cannot be faulted for having stationed troops at the prison, for popular riots were an increasingly serious danger. But as fate or governmental ineptitude would have it, the incident served to increase Wilkes' popularity and the general discontent. The ministry feared that English troops might have misdirected sympathies and therefore sent a Scottish detachment, which was hated by the English mob first for their nationality and second for being countrymen of Bute.

Just before several soldiers were made to stand trial for the death of Allen, Junius attacked the ministry under another name, "Fiat Justitia." Secretary of War Barrington — Philip Francis' superior in the War Office — had responded to the killings by congratulating the troops for their "zeal and good behaviour." To the commanding officer Barrington wrote, "I have great pleasure in informing you that his Majesty highly approved of the conduct of both the officers and men," and promised "every defence and protection" in the case of any "disagreeable circumstance," no doubt meaning the trial for murder. In his letter Junius makes the substance of Barrington's letter public, attacks him for his "very improper and indecent" use of the king's name, and argues that the promise of protection and support is unconstitutional. The Junius letter is spirited and pointed but owes its greatest effect to Barrington's letter, which damned itself in the eyes of many Londoners.

A Wilkes partisan named Clarke died in a later election riot, perhaps killed by a ruffian, McQuirk, who had been hired by the ministerial forces. McQuirk was sentenced by a jury to death, but after a reexamination of the evidence, which was ambiguous, the king "thought proper to extend Our royal mercy" to the Irishman. Junius entered the fray by goading the people to take this as an insult to trial by jury and to the struggle for popular liberty. The letter cleverly contrasts this pardon to the more notable avoidance of pardon in the case of Wilkes: "Now, my Lord [Grafton], let me ask you, Has it never occurred to your Grace, while you were withdrawing this desperate wretch from ... justice, ... that there is another man, who is the favourite of his country, whose pardon would have been accepted with gratitude, whose pardon would have healed all our divisions?... Is it to murderers only that you will extend the mercy of the crown?" (pp. 57–58). Wilkes, no longer in Junius' eyes the outlaw, the leader of riots, or the destroyer of free elections, is now portrayed as the healer of "all our divisions." Junius seems to have completely reversed his position on Wilkes, though in fact he makes no mention of Wilkes' character. Junius' underlying consistency is found in his antipathy toward the Grafton ministry. Whereas the ministry was earlier blamed for Wilkes' freedom, it is now blamed for his imprisonment.

The king, with his personal grudge against Wilkes, urged the ministry to take further action against him. But their next step backfired even worse than the previous step. Without considering the consequences, they decided to expel Wilkes from Parliament. A majority was easily persuaded; hence his expulsion, of dubious justice, on February 3, 1769, for "Number 45," the volume of obscene poetry, and a publication on the St. George's Fields incident. On February 16 a reelection was held and Wilkes was unanimously elected. The next day Parliament declared Wilkes incapable of being a member. On March 16 a third election was held and, the court party candidate Dingley receiving no support and much abuse, Wilkes was again reelected unanimously. Parliament accordingly declared the election void, ordered a new one and this time found a candidate to run against Wilkes, one Colonel Henry Lawes Luttrell.

Three days before the April 13 election — the fourth — a Junius letter appeared in the *Public Advertiser* addressed to Grafton. The minister is chastised for pardoning McQuirk, supporting "the miserable Dingley," basely deserting his former friend Wilkes, and driving the country to distress. In explicit contrast to the earlier Grafton, Junius professes no admiration for Wilkes' character — "I have frequently censured Mr. Wilkes' character" — and argues rightly that the Wilkes case had become a constitutional issue. At the election, the court party made every effort to defeat their opponent. But Wilkes — still in prison for libel and blasphemy — received 1,143 votes, while Luttrell mustered only 296. Parliament promptly declared Luttrell the winner! The angry freeholders of Middlesex then petititioned the House of Commons to reverse their decision, but after a great debate beginning at one o'clock in the afternoon of May 8 and lasting until four o'clock the next morning, the House rejected the petition — and Wilkes — by a vote of 221 to 152. Parliament was then prorogued until January, 1770.

The questions raised by the Middlesex election, however, were far from settled. The debate raged on in a spirit of crisis. Burke wrote of the "present discontents" in 1770,

That government is at once dreaded and contemned; that the laws are despoiled of all their respected and salutary terrors; that their inaction is a subject of ridicule, and their exertion of abhorrence; that rank, and office and title, and all the solemn plausibilities of the world, have lost their reverence and effect; ...that hardly anything above or below, abroad or at home, is sound and entire; but that disconnection and confusion, in offices, in parties, in families, in Parliament, in the nation, prevail beyond the disorders of any former time: these are facts universally admitted and lamented.[5]

To Junius the Middlesex controversy involved "the greatest constitutional question, that has arisen since the revolution" (p. 177). Adherents of the court party could not deny the crisis, though they could deny its legitimacy. "Nothing," wrote Samuel Johnson, "is necessary, at this *alarming crisis,* but to consider the alarm as false."[6]

The court party's position on Luttrell versus Wilkes was most ably argued by Johnson (in *The False Alarm),* Chief Justice Mansfield, and Blackstone (author of the famous *Commentaries).* The issue turned essentially on the view one took of the power of Parliament vis-à-vis the power of the crown or the people. The anti-Wilkites maintained that the Commons was free to determine its composition without coercion from above (the crown) or below (the electorate). The House might yield to advice and pressure but ultimately the power was theirs, without appeal. In this case the electorate was trying to coerce them to accept Wilkes contrary to their ruling. Blackstone, who published a refutation of Junius, maintained that a general incapacity to sit in the House of Commons could be created only by an act of Parliament, but an incapacity limited to a single session (as in the case of Wilkes) could be created by the Commons alone. Thus the expulsion lasted through the entire session, invalidating Wilkes' reelections, but would not be in effect at the next general election. After Wilkes' first expulsion any vote cast for him was invalid or void and so had no effect on votes cast for other candidates. Since Luttrell received the greatest number of *legal* votes, he was the victor. Without this power to enforce it, an expulsion would be no punishment at all, and Parliament ought to have the right, as Johnson said, to expel "enormously bad" men. There was even a precedent for this position: in 1711 Robert Walpole was expelled for alleged corruption, reelected, and then declared incapable of sitting in that Parliament.

Because of the cumulative and indefinite nature of the English constitution, however, the issue could not be definitively solved by authority, even if it were not accompanied by riots and passion. Equally illustrious men — among them Burke and Chatham — argued the opposing position that Wilkes had been legally reelected and should be seated. Junius fanned the flames of contention by attacking personalities, refuting Blackstone, bringing forward new arguments and reiterating old ones, and proclaiming the importance of the issue to English liberty. He was always careful to dissociate the issue from Wilkes himself. If Wilkes were an "enormously bad" man, that had nothing to do with the matter. Two years after Parliament had tried to settle the crisis Junius had not given up: "I need not make you any excuse for endeavouring to keep alive the attention of the public to the decision of the Middlesex election. The more I consider it, the more I am convinced that, as a *fact,* it is indeed highly injurious to the rights of the people; but that, as a *precedent,* it is one of the most dangerous that ever was established against those who are to come after us" (p. 241). The "common right of every subject of the realm is invaded" by the decision; the time may come "when not only a single person, but a whole county, and in effect the entire collective body of the people may again be robbed of their birthright by a vote of the house of commons" (pp. 97, 93).

Junius tried to keep the issue very simple but, with a thorny issue debated by minds as subtle as Burke's and Blackstone's, this was a difficult and perhaps impossible task. When his opponents cited precedents and legal analyses, however, one of Junius' tactics was to scorn their "subtleties and refinements" (pp. 98, 99) and assert instead that no lawyers were needed to "decide for me upon a plain constitutional question" (p. 78). But, on the other hand, the issue as Junius saw it was essentially an intellectual one and therefore all the more consequential. The "evidence of the senses," to which Junius continually appeals, might well gravitate toward evidence of Wilkes' profligacy rather than evidence of lost freedom for future generations. Thus to some extent he had to meet the lawyers on their own ground.

Junius does not dispute Parliament's right to expulsion, but he holds the popular right of election to be inviolate. It is, he said, the "birthright" of every Englishman. By rejecting the candidate with the majority of votes, the Commons had deprived him of this right and, if unchallenged, might do the same to any Englishman. Although Blackstone argued the government case, his *Commentaries* specified exactly what could disqualify a man from this right, and Wilkes was clearly not disqualified. (Blackstone later altered the passage.) "For the defence of truth, of law, and reason," Junius gibed, "the Doctor's book [that is, the *Commentaries*] may be safely consulted; but whoever wishes to cheat a neighbour of his estate, or to rob a country of its rights, need make no scruple of consulting the Doctor himself" (p. 78). He denied any "legal incapacity" for Wilkes' reelection on the grounds that no statute existed which applied to Wilkes' case. The Walpole precedent was not to the point: Walpole had been denied his seat for a specific crime; Wilkes was denied his only on the grounds of expulsion. Furthermore, Walpole's opponent (unlike Luttrell) was denied the seat, which then remained vacant. It was never given to a candidate who did not receive the majority vote. When the House of Commons under George III accepted a candidate whom the people had rejected, they corrupted and vitiated their entire body. "They have rejected the majority of votes, the only criterion, by which our laws judge of the sense of the people; they have transferred the right of election from the collective to the representative body; and by these acts, taken separately or together, they have essentially altered the original constitution of the house of commons" (p. 171).

During the course of three years, Junius moved from being contemptuous of Wilkes to being an outspoken and persuasive supporter and even, by correspondence, a friend and advisor. But in

truth there was less change in attitude than there appears to be.
Junius always had a singularly clearheaded view of Wilkes' moral
shortcomings, his degree of natural ability, and the constitutional
issues attached to, though distinct from, Wilkes the man. Usually
Junius avoided the issue of Wilkes' personality as irrelevant. But
Wilkes' character was so bad that even his opponents overlooked
it. In his anti-Wilkes pamphlet Johnson wrote that "lampoon itself
would disdain to speak ill of him of whom no man speaks well."[7]
Despite this, Wilkes was undoubtedly a man of great personal appeal to many men — not merely the mob — and a potent symbol of
popular liberty. It is to Junius' credit that this appeal did not
obscure a just estimate of Wilkes' importance. Just after the fourth
Middlesex election Junius wrote to the duke of Grafton that "Mr.
Wilkes, if not persecuted, will soon be forgotten" (p. 67), and four
months before his prison sentence was out Junius urged the king to
pardon him for the same reason: "Pardon this man the remainder
of his punishment, and if resentment still prevails, make it, what it
should have been long since, an act, not of mercy, but contempt.
He will soon fall back into his natural station, a silent senator, and
hardly supporting the weekly eloquence of a newspaper. The gentle
breath of peace would leave him on the surface, neglected and
unremoved. It is only the tempest, that lifts him from his place"
(pp. 171–72). The king, however, was not so wise. His obsession
with "the destruction of one man" was, as Junius said, "an ill-
advised, unworthy personal resentment." Wilkes' persecution
became his reward, at the expense of the government: "Animated
by the favour of the people on one side, and heated by persecution
on the other, his views and sentiments changed with his situation.
Hardly serious at first, he is now an enthusiast" (p. 163).

III   *City Politics*

Since the government insisted on persecuting Wilkes, his
popularity and success continued. While still in prison he was
elected a London alderman and was responsible for the formation
of an important new radical movement of "patriots," the Society
of Supporters of the Bill of Rights. In 1771 he was elected sheriff
and in 1774 lord mayor of London and member of Parliament. Far
from being a dangerous demagogue as a member, he did little,
behaved respectably, and was chiefly concerned with vindicating
his own character. When the Whigs came into power at the close of

the American War they erased the precedent of the Middlesex election from the records of the House of Commons.

As alderman of London Wilkes is of some importance in the career of Junius because of the private correspondence between the two men. Furthermore, the city — apart from Wilkes — was, like Junius, in radical opposition to the government during these years. On June 24, 1769, two months after Luttrell was seated for Middlesex, the freemen of London met and began to take control of the city government from the hands of court sympathizers and place it in the hands of the opposition. The election of James Townsend and John Sawbridge as sheriffs was the start of official city activities much more radical than had been seen for generations. At the same meeting the freemen approved a petition to the king charging the king's ministers with the crimes which Junius was also condemning: invading trial by jury, issuing general warrants, evading habeas corpus, murdering the people with troops, robbing the people of their right to election, and so on. The petition was carried to the king and presented with great ceremony. The king received it, handed it unopened to the lord in waiting, turned his back on the deputation, and began a conversation with the Danish minister.

Eight months later the petition was still unanswered. In the meantime Londoners had chosen a radical lord mayor in William Beckford, a supporter of Chatham, father of the novelist, and one of the richest men in England. Under Beckford's leadership they prepared an even stronger antiministerial remonstrance to the king. The king was understandably not eager to receive it and when asked about the presentation, he replied, "As the case is entirely new, I will take time to consider of it . . . ." Junius, who entirely supported such petitions, found the reply offensive: "For a King of Great Britain to take Time to consider, whether he will or will not receive a Petition from his Subjects, seems to me to amount to this, that he will take Time to consider whether he will or will not adhere to the . . . Declaration of Rights" (p. 472). The remonstrance was presented on March 14 to the king, who with some justice declared it "disrespectful to me, injurious to my parliament, and irreconcilable to the principles of the constitution."

The king's formal reply won the applause of the court party and of many moderates who were repelled by the radical remonstrance. This led Junius to devote two bold letters of vehement attack on the king's answer in an effort to disparage the reply and to widen support for the remonstrance from the city to the entire nation. He argued that the reply "threatens to punish the subject for exercising a privilege, hitherto undisputed, of petitioning the crown," that "it is not a direct answer to the petition of the city," and that its assertions are "absolutely unsupported, either in argument or fact" (pp. 182, 184). Along with reasoned support of his position he deftly mingled ridicule of the establishment: "Our gracious King indeed is abundantly civil to himself. Instead of an answer to a petition, his majesty very gracefully pronounces his own panegyric" (p. 184). Throughout both letters there is a call for more petitions from "all parts of the kingdom," a call which was in fact taken up and which led to a stream of petitions to the king. Many leaders of the opposition, like George Grenville (whom Junius never attacked), were hostile to the city attacks on the government. But Junius exacerbated the crisis by praising the people and dropping threats of rebellion against the king.

Antiministerial sentiment was widespread but often rendered ineffectual by the failure of the opposition to work together. Junius occasionally tried to intercede to pacify warring factions among the London radicals, but his talents were ill-suited to peacemaking.

With Wilkes in prison, the leadership of the radical cause fell to Beckford and to a Brentford vicar, John Horne, later known as Horne Tooke. Horne began the Bill of Rights Society initially to support Wilkes and pay his debts, but when Wilkes left prison the two feuded. Horne, with the wealthiest and most respectable members, left the club to form another, the Constitutional Society. To no advantage of the cause or themselves, they washed their dirty linen in public in an exchange collected as *The Controversial Letters of Wilkes and Horne.* In a private letter to his cousin, Philip Francis wrote scornfully of this "open war in the newspapers." "Nothing can be more contemptible, in my opinion, nor less interesting than the whole of their correspondence. Horne's malice and rancour are mean and wretched beyond all description."[8]

In the shrievalty election of July, 1771, Horne refused to endorse Wilkes, preferring another defector from the Bill of Rights Society. Wilkes and his running mate led the poll, however, followed by two court party men, and Horne's candidate finished last. Junius then launched an attack on Horne which he probably intended as an isolated attack, but Horne, an excellent controversialist, came to his own defense and led Junius into a series of anti-Horne letters. Junius' ploy was to argue that Horne, in opposing Wilkes, had therefore gone to the side of the court party and found a "new zeal in support of administration." The accusation that Horne was intentionally serving the court party was almost certainly false. Horne was an ardent antiministerial agitator and his candidate had no connections with the court party. But such was the passion and distrust of the times that the charge could be made and taken seriously. Francis makes the same charge: "I really suspect that the ministry pay [Horne] for what he does."[9] Horne armed himself for extended combat and, in a letter to Junius in the *Public Advertiser,* demanded an explanation in a way not to be denied.

Assuming a pretense, at least, of not wanting to exacerbate the split among radicals, Junius wrote Horne a personal letter which began, "I cannot descend to an altercation with you in the newspapers" (p. 256). But he did not spare Horne. Indeed, he had been goaded into a consuming rage which had never before been so fully exposed in a Junius letter. At the close of the letter Junius said it was "not intended for the public" but gave Horne permission to publish it if he so desired, which he promptly did. It is curious to observe Philip Francis' delight at this arrangement. By his testimony the attack on Horne was far more important than unifying the conflicting factions. In his capacity as mere reader of the newspapers, Francis wrote that "Junius has given Horne a most severe correction. The best on't is, that Junius, under pretense of writing Horne a *private* letter, makes him the *editor* of the grossest and most infamous libel that ever was published. This I take to be a *coup d'état.* Wouldn't you laugh if you saw the parson in the pillory for publishing a letter, in which he himself is virtually abused? Horne's credit is very low indeed."[10]

Horne soon published a lengthy rebuttal. The public correspondence continued through several letters, Junius perhaps having exposed himself more than he intended and Horne having done honorable battle with the most dreaded epistolary antagonist of the time. The engagement offered a display of astonishing invective from Junius but totally failed in his dubious attempt to restore unity within the cause.

Though much more amicable toward Wilkes, Junius often differed with him in private letters. In all, some seventeen letters passed between these two extraordinary molders of public opinion, Wilkes and Junius. When he began the correspondence Junius promised that "it must always make part of *Junius's* plan to support Mr. Wilkes, while *he* makes common cause with the people"

(p. 398). Wilkes was not a noble man dedicated primarily to political goals, though he often found himself in that role. His motives were more likely personal than political; "I was never a Wilkite," he told the king. But Wilkes' political sense — whatever its motives — was with the cause of the people and therefore agreeable to Junius. In a public letter Junius stated a general principle that he worked from: "If individuals have no virtues, their vices may be of use to us. I care not with what principle the new-born patriot is animated, if the measures he supports are beneficial to the community" (p. 297). Wilkes had some virtues along with his vices and Junius was willing to avail himself of both. Junius was no Wilkite either; rather it appears that with considerable perspicacity Junius abused or used "that devil Wilkes" to promote his own political ends.

CHAPTER 4

The Sport of His Fury

W HEN Junius was at the peak of his power, Edmund Burke paid tribute to him — and furthered his own attack on the ministry — in a speech to the House of Commons:

How comes this Junius to have broke through the cobwebs of the law? The myrmidons of the court have been long, and are still, pursuing him in vain. They will not spend their time upon me, or you, or you. No: they disdain such vermin, when the mighty boar of the forest, that has broke through all their toils, is before them. But what will all their efforts avail? No sooner has he wounded one than he lays down another dead at his feet. . . . King, lords, and commons are but the sport of his fury. Were he a member of this house, what might not be expected from his knowledge, his firmness, and integrity? He would be easily known by his contempt of all danger, by his penetration, by his vigour. Nothing would escape his vigilance and activity. Bad ministers could conceal nothing from his sagacity; nor could promises nor threats induce him to conceal anything from the public.[1]

With his awesome power, the "mighty boar of the forest" sported with wide-ranging issues and the most formidable individuals: he did not heed the call to criticize only "measures, not men."

The first letter that appeared with the signature of Junius, on November 21, 1768, was concerned with the prime issue of the time — the Wilkes controversy. Sometime after this initial letter, however, Junius apparently decided to make a concerted attack on the ministry under his new cognito rather than under a series of names like "Corregio," "C.," "Lucius," "Atticus," and the like. Two months after the November letter, a comprehensive attack on the ministry — both the men and the measures — launched Junius as the formidable combatant whose attacks would be general as well as particular, but all calculated toward one end: destroying the present ministry. When Junius prepared a collected edition of his letters, this broad attack on the ministry appeared to be an appropriate beginning; thus it was made Letter I. The previous letter was quietly forgotten, though the issue it treated reappeared often in subsequent letters. The breadth and artifice of Letter I suggest a conscious design on the part of Junius to begin a systematic, unified attack on the ministry in a series of letters. The ministry's handling of the Wilkes controversy was to be only one of many of Junius' targets, but all of his attacks are based on a single idea which provides coherence to the letters and justification for their rhetoric.

I   *Junius' Thesis*

In the late 1760s there was a pervasive sense of crisis in England, growing out of the Wilkes affair but by no means limited to it. A pamphlet of 1768 written by George Grenville, head of the ministry from 1763 to 1765, and William Knox cataloged the alarming ills in *The Present State of the Nation:*

No reverence for the customs or opinions of our ancestors, no attachment but to private interest, nor any zeal but for selfish gratifications.... An impoverished and heavily-burthened public. A declining trade and decreasing specie. A people luxurious and licentious, impatient of rule, and despising all authority. Government relaxed in every sinew, and a corrupt selfish spirit pervading the whole. The state destitute of alliances, and without respect from foreign nations. A powerful combination, anxious for an occasion to retrieve their honour and wreak their vengeance....[2]

Grenville was the only minister of whom Junius consistently spoke well, and Junius clearly admired this pamphlet. There are significant differences between the views of Grenville and Junius, but Junius adopted a thesis, arguments, and even some evidence from *The Present State.*

England had not been at war since the Peace of Paris in 1763. Nevertheless, the price of the Seven Years War had been high, and the ensuing peace was marred by a large national debt and accompanying interest. The authors of *The Present State* thought that this was a key to the present discontents, and Junius, writing under the name of Atticus, at first agreed with them. Despite the successes of the late war, he argued, Great Britain contained "in itself an interior principle of weakness and decay ... the operation of which is not less certain than fatal" (Wade, II, 203). When the war was in progress England could control the seas and trade effectively, but with the coming of peace and competition from other nations she could not maintain her superiority. Thus she began a serious decline, not only in the economy but in national strength and morale. "It is agreed on all hands," Atticus wrote, "that we are in no condition to meet a war. Our enemies know and presume upon it.... They know the miserable state of our finances, the distraction and weakness of our government, and above all, the alarming differences which threaten a rupture with our colonies" (Wade, II, 204–05). The nation had peaked in success and prosperity during the Seven Years War and now, less than ten years later, it was suffering an alarming decline which, if not checked, would prove fatal.

As time passed Junius did not become more sanguine. He moved away from Atticus' early position that the cause was chiefly economic, but he felt more and more strongly that the nation was suffering a worsening crisis. Instead of viewing the ministry as being incompetent in economics, he increasingly saw it as being incompetent in politics in the largest sense. Indeed, the ministry and king seemed bent on subverting the constitution. The only hope Junius perceived was to change the policy of the king and destroy the ministry. Only by replacing the present corrupt ministry with a great man, in combination with other men of principle, could the country be saved.

Both Junius' manner and his matter indicate that he believed himself to be witnessing the English nation in decline. The decline was not its inevitable historical course but was caused by inept, corrupt government. "Individuals perish by their own imprudence," said Atticus, "and the ruin of an empire is no more than the misconduct of a minister or a king" (Wade, II, 254). In such a crisis, "the English nation must be rouzed, and put upon its guard" (p. 205). This was the task Junius set for himself.

He succeeded in rousing the nation but not in saving it. The great man did not appear; the men of principle did not combine. Junius' view of the Grafton ministry and the king became even darker. When Grafton was finally dismissed, his replacement, Lord North, was no improvement. As North's position became more secure, Junius had less cause to write because he had less chance of success. In his last letter to Woodfall, after he had ended his career as political writer, Junius was despondent and without hope: "In the present state of things, if I were to write again, I must be as silly as any of the horned Cattle, that run mad through the City.... I meant the Cause & the public. Both are given up. I feel for the honour of this Country, when I see that there are not ten men in it, who will unite & stand together upon any one question. But it is all alike, vile & contemptible" (p. 393). During the course of the letters Junius' basic view of the nation does not change except to become more pessimistic.

When one notices how clearly this view is set forth in Letter I and how the initial attack is managed, it is difficult to believe that Francis created Junius to be simply one more political letter writer who would address himself sporadically to transitory issues as they arose. He seems to have had a larger design and more formidable existence in mind. Letter I is no ordinary political letter; it differs considerably even from Francis' earlier non-Junian letters. Its comprehensive view of the state of the nation, its forthrightness in assigning the general cause of the discontents, its polished style, and especially the nature of its specific attacks — short and inflammatory, suggesting real corruption without definitively supporting it — all suggest that this was intended as an initial foray in an intended war, not the entire campaign.

The letter conveys a vision of pervasive disorder. After an exordium on the free Englishman's loyalty and "rational attachment" to his government when the national interest is being protected, Junius begins his attack in a tone of firm moderation. "The situation of this country is alarming enough to rouse the attention of every man, who pretends to a concern for the public welfare. Appearances justify suspicion; and, when the safety of a nation is at stake, suspicion is a just ground of enquiry. Let us enter into it with candour and decency" (p. 26). The firmness remains throughout the letter, but the moderation soon gives way to strong uncompromising attack. His catalog of evils — "an universal spirit of distrust and dissatisfaction, a rapid decay of trade, dissensions in all parts of the empire, and a total loss of respect in the eyes of foreign power" — is similar to that in *The Present State,* but the judgment is harsher: the government is "weak, distracted, and corrupt." For Junius the cause of these discontents is unmistakably "the pernicious brand of government," or more precisely, the ministry. "Perhaps there never was an instance of a change, in the circumstances and temper of a whole nation, so sudden and extraordinary as that which the misconduct of ministers has, within these few years, produced in Great Britain."

Not only does Junius clearly assert in Letter I the thesis of the collected *Letters,* he also assumes what was to be his characteristic role as public examiner and accuser. He surveys the character of the ministry and finds incompetent, inexperienced ministers mismanaging the finances; governors alienating the colonies; secretaries of state ineptly chosen; a "servile, humiliating . . . courtier" in charge of the military; and the chief criminal judge "a traitor to the public" (p. 32). For the next three years Junius would expand and elaborate on this survey. The thesis stated and his ethos established, Junius ends his initial letter with a rhetorical tour de force, comprehending in one grand sweep the ills of the nation and the state of her people:

In one view behold a nation overwhelmed with debt; her revenues wasted; her trade declining; the affections of her colonies alienated; the duty of the magistrate transferred to the soldiery; a gallant army, which never fought unwillingly but against their fellow subjects, mouldering away for want of the direction of a man of common abilities and spirit; and, in the last instance, the administration of justice become odious and suspected to the whole body of the people. This deplorable scene admits of but one addition — that we are governed by counsels, from which a reasonable man can expect no remedy but poison, no relief but death. (p. 33)

The stage is set for three years of concerted effort to destroy the ministry and alter the policy of the king. There only remained the task of establishing, and keeping, a large readership.

II *The Sacrificial Nobleman*

The initial statement of thesis, made vigorously, compactly, and with a convincing indignation, was specific enough to damn ministers individually and general enough to persuade the nation of pervasive corruption. It opened a beehive of controversy which could allow Junius, secure in his anonymity, to proceed freely in his criticism and invective as the circumstances moved him. One brilliant attack alone, however, could not firmly establish a reputation and readership. They must be formed on successive letters equally dynamic, controversial, and effective. How Junius planned to meet this challenge we cannot be certain, but it is not unlikely that he expected a government writer to defend the ministry by undertaking to answer his attacks. For Junius such a response would have two merits: it would fan the flame of controversy, exciting a public interest in his own writing, and it would provide him with a particular antagonist — although probably an anonymous one — upon whom Junius could sharpen his ministerial attack. The event proved to be far superior to this, however. The response to Junius came not from an anonymous governmental writer but from a nobleman, high military officer, and scholar — Sir William Draper. Draper intended to demolish Junius, but the outcome was otherwise: Draper became Junius' sacrificial lamb, a victim who unwittingly offered himself for slaughter to establish the fame and glory which Junius needed in order to be effective in the more important task which he had set for himself.

Of the total of sixty-nine letters in the collected Junius letters, ten of them concern Sir William Draper; five are written by Draper and five by Junius. Draper was not a man of great importance in political affairs. He was, however, a man of considerable distinction who had achieved fame as a general by leading a successful attack on the Spanish in the Philippine Islands. Manila was taken and the promise of a large ransom received, but Spain later refused to honor it. For his services Draper was awarded the Order of the Bath by the king, approbation by the public, and a comfortable income which allowed him to retire to his estate near Bath. He was also blessed with an excellent education, close ties with a university, and literary talent which he often employed in political debate.

Draper was indignant over Junius' harsh attack on his friend and military superior, the marquis of Granby, master-general of the ordnance. Since Junius' plan was to discredit the entire ministry, he had attacked Granby as well as the more likely targets such as Grafton, but Granby was probably the most popular member of the administration. In Letter I Junius had granted his courage but charged him with "a total absence of all feeling and reflection" (p. 31), with nepotism, with a servile behavior, and with an obsessive concern for dispensing commissions. Ignoring Junius' attacks on the other ministers, Draper rushed to Granby's defense: "A very long, uninterrupted, impartial, I will add, a most disinterested friendship with Lord Granby, gives me the right to affirm, that all Junius's assertions are false and scandalous" (p. 35). Why did Junius take up Draper's challenge and devote a subsequent portion of the *Letters* to him? He could easily have ignored Draper, just as he ignored many other attackers. The most important reasons have already been suggested: to hold on to and enlarge his audience and to establish a reputation for literary and political finesse. In addition, an exchange with Draper would offer opportunities to further his attacks on the ministry.

It is revealing to observe Junius' strategy in this exchange. He had several advantages. Draper had attacked first and voluntarily; therefore, Junius could deny responsibility for whatever injuries might come from the exchange. Furthermore, Draper was famous and would, therefore, attract attention to Junius, and he also had literary talent, though not so much that he could match Junius. There were disadvantages, however, but they were not formidable enough to offset the appeal of the challenge. The disadvantages lay in the personalities: Granby, with his popularity, was not a promising means for arousing public hatred for the ministry, and Draper himself was hardly despicable. Junius, therefore, decided on a technical tour de force, an arresting, dazzling display of his literary and political talent that would make itself felt by an unmistakable victory over the epistolary challenger Draper.

To achieve this end, Junius used three important techniques. First, he relentlessly fixed on Draper's weakest arguments and exposed their fatuity, which by implication damned all of Draper's logic. For example, in his initial letter, Draper tried to counter Junius' argument that the ministry was responsible for the evils of the nation by charging that "Junius, and such writers as himself, occasion all the mischiefs complained of, by falsely and maliciously traducing the best characters in the kingdom" (p. 34). Draper's passion had betrayed him into extremes — "all" and "best" — which make the assertion literally fatuous, no matter how much truth it might contain. Junius replied with cool superiority: "And do you really think, Sir William, that the licentious pen of a political writer is able to produce such important effects? A little calm reflection might have shewn you, that national calamities do not arise from the description, but from the real character and conduct of ministers" (p. 39). And he continued by offering gratuitous advice to his erring opponent on how to conduct a political argument. Second, he defended his attack on Granby by reasserting it, then by moving from the dubious personal attack to the larger issue of the decrepitude of the military (which would be harder for Draper to contradict convincingly), by skillfully sidestepping and ignoring Draper's attempt to pursue the issue of Granby, by claiming — with considerable justice — that Draper himself was responsible for eliciting a more damning attack on Granby than Junius originally intended, and by claiming, in a tone of supreme confidence, a victory on the issue which in fact a tally of arguments and proofs would not confirm.

The third technique, however, was the most telling — a series of innuendos made by directing interrogations at Draper. The retired general, Junius suggests, accepted a bribe to be silent about the Manila ransom: perhaps his knighthood, the regiment which he later sold, or his commission as Irish colonel which provides half-pay for his duties. Junius' financial probes were especially telling, for the common arrangements for military men were at best un-savory. Draper felt compelled to defend himself, which made mat-ters worse for him. The effect was crushing. By his third letter Draper was entirely on the defensive. He confessed that Junius was "putting my life and conduct to the rack" and ended with sputter-ing invective: "You bite against a file: cease viper" (p. 50). Junius had clearly succeeded in attracting an audience, displaying his intel-lectual superiority, and humiliating his adversary. From his lofty height he bade adieu to Sir William by drawing the moral: "From the lessons I have given you, you may collect a profitable instruc-tion for your future life. They will either teach you so to regulate your conduct, as to be able to set the most malicious inquiries at de-fiance; or, if that be a lost hope, they will teach you prudence enough not to attract the public attention to a character, which will only pass without censure, when it passes without observation" (pp. 52–53).

Six months later Draper discovered that the correspondence had been republished in book form. He was indignant, entered the lists again, denouncing Junius as a tyrant and throwing out dark chal-lenges to a duel. But there was no real contest. Junius remained in complete control and Draper was defamed even further. In his last appearance (Letter XXVII) Draper is a mere tool in Junius' hands, being skillfully used to attack the duke of Bedford.

III   The King and King's Friends

The success which the mysterious letter writer had against his noble challenger announced unequivocally that a major political element had appeared which must be heard and reckoned with. But, as Letter I indicated, Junius was not to be content with humili-ating lesser game like Sir William Draper and Lord Granby. His eye was on more impressive targets — no less than the king of England, his court friends, and his ministers.

Junius' expressed attitude toward the king is sometimes one of apparent respect, sometimes ironic attack, and sometimes of open contempt. But, whatever is actually said in the letters, however thin the line between irony and straightforwardness in his allusions to "our gracious king," there can be no doubt that Junius heartily detested George III. His attacks on the king were less forceful than usual because he did not want to endanger his printer, Woodfall, or alienate his audience. The danger of exposing "a simple printer," he said in a letter to Wilkes, "will account for my abstaining from the King so long, & for the undeserved Moderation, with which I have treated him. I know my ground thoroughly when I affirm, that *he alone* is the Mark. It is not Bute, nor even the Princess Dowager. It is the odious hypocrite himself [the king] whom every honest Man should detest, and every brave man should attack" (p. 430). A stronger attack on the king of England — whose person and office were traditionally given respect, no matter how many faults could be found — does not often find its way into print. Junius well knew the necessity for confining to private letters sentiments as harsh and bitter as these.

When George III came to the throne in 1760, he was received with overwhelming enthusiasm: a young, attractive, English — not German — king, who "gloried in the name of Briton," was an engaging novelty. He appeared to be a pious, dignified, affectionate man who could command the respect of his people. When he died, sixty years later, he had suffered from a disease mistaken for insanity for two decades and England had passed through a period of profound change. They had been years of unstable or controversial ministries; the commonwealth had been disrupted and the American colonies lost in a deplorable war; the security of the nation had been threatened first by the ideas of the French Revolution, then by the Napoleonic Wars; and an economic revolution had begun which would change the entire society.

What, then, does one make of George III? His character and his intentions, especially during the early years of his reign, have excited several conflicting theories among the historians, and the puzzle remains today. One theory, the Tory defense of George III, was advanced by contemporary friends of the court and by the historian John Adolphus in 1802. According to Adolphus, the first two Georges, being foreigners, were in no position to rule by themselves and so lost much of their power to the Whig oligarchy. When George III ascended the throne, he determined to recover the royal powers which had been usurped by the ministers. Thus the king in-

tended to institute a new system, an admirable and entirely constitutional plan. He wanted to reassert the power of the monarchy in
accordance with the Revolutionary Settlement and rid the system of
corruption, the basis of power for the Whig connections.

A second theory, prominent among mid-nineteenth-century historians and later, agrees that George planned to institute a new system, but with the difference that he wanted more power than the
king could constitutionally have. In his monumental history of the
eighteenth century, W. E. H. Lecky asserts that George III "in-
flicted more profound and enduring injuries upon his country than
any other modern English king. Ignorant, narrow-minded, and arbitrary, with an unbounded confidence in his own judgment and an
extravagant estimate of his prerogative, ... he spent a long life in
obstinately resisting measures which are now almost universally admitted to have been good, and in supporting measures which are as
universally admitted to have been bad."[3] The root of the problem,
in Lecky's opinion, was the king's determination to increase royal
prerogative.

A school of modern historians led by Sir Lewis Namier denies
that a Whig oligarchy had usurped royal power, that George II was
a "king in bondage," that the ministries' power was based on corruption, or that George III had any ideas about establishing a new
system when he ascended the throne. The alleged new system, they
argue, was the result of there being no heir apparent to the throne
about whom disappointed politicians could gather. In the absence
of this the politicians were forced by their neurotic fears — as in the
case of Newcastle — or their self-interest to justify their resistance
to the king by false legends.[4] The basic issues at stake in this controversy are crucial to an understanding of Junius. Although it is
impossible to explore the complexities of each theory or pass judgment on them here, they may serve to locate Junius' attitude
toward the king within the larger spectrum of possible attitudes. In
fact, the first well-developed appearance of the second theory, in
Burke's *Thoughts on the Cause of the Present Discontents,* had a
very great influence on Junius.

Before the appearance of Burke's *Thoughts* in April, 1770,
Junius' expressed attitudes toward the king were different in tone
and substance than they were thereafter. Having observed Junius'
rhetorical manipulation of his subjects in the Wilkes affair, one
should not be surprised to find apparent changes of heart with
respect to the king. Before assuming the name Junius, he posed as

defender of the king to attack the ministry: the "great person" had been "wantonly and treasonably attacked" by Wilkes, "the King's person" and his subjects were "at the mercy of a licentious, drunken rabble," and the ministers did nothing to stop the "horror and outrage" (Wade, II, 165–66). No irony, no crocodile tears are in evidence. In Letter I of the collected letters, however, where Junius so carefully charts his course, his praise of the king is accompanied by a subtle yet unmistakable current of irony and ridicule. Having damned the government as "weak, distracted, and corrupt," he turns to the king: "When our gracious sovereign ascended the throne, we were a flourishing and a contented people" — no compliment to *this* king except a conventional "gracious." His "idea of uniting all parties, of trying all characters, and distributing the offices of state by rotation" — referring to the frequent changes of ministry — "was gracious and benevolent to an extreme," an assertion which could almost be taken seriously by a not-too-careful reader, were it not for the Swiftian afterthought: "though it has not yet produced the many salutary effects which were intended by it." In the context, Junius' defense of the king — that his plan contains no "folly," no "capricious partiality to new faces," no "natural turn for low intrigue," no "treacherous amusement of double and triple negociations" — is more suggestive than convincing. The irony becomes heavier — "No, Sir, it arose from a continued anxiety, in the purest of all possible hearts, for the general welfare" — and the truth becomes painful: "Unfortunately for us, the event has not been answerable to the design. After a rapid succession of changes, we are reduced to that state, which hardly any change can mend" (pp. 26–27). In this letter the direct attack is on the ministry, but the king by no means escapes unscathed. After this irony, no later references to the king as "a character truly gracious and benevolent" can be read as unadulterated praise.

The ironic ambience which plays around the word "gracious" becomes a Junian trademark, though it is certainly a mild, even gentle, form of criticism for Junius. As time passes and the state of the nation worsens, in Junius' view, the attack escalates to bold phrases like "treachery of a minister, or the abused simplicity of a king" (p. 62) and to the famous "Address to the King" in Letter XXXV, but there is still a profession of respect toward a king who is partially the victim of evil ministers.

At about this time Burke published his long pamphlet, *Thoughts on the Cause of the Present Discontents,* arguing a position that added weight to Junius' attacks. The "present discontents" of the title indicates that Burke was no friend of the administration; he believed there was "something ... amiss in the constitution, or in the conduct of government."⁵ To dramatize the danger and the need for his solution, Burke created a "legend" — as Sir Lewis Namier has called it — about a plot designed to abolish parties or "connections" and establish a dominant power in the crown, effectively separating it from the Parliament and the people. The plan was to be effected by establishing a double cabinet — one, the ministry, which would ostensibly make policy and be responsible for it, and the other, a group of favorites called the king's men or king's friends, which would secretly manipulate the ministry and policy to gain power for the crown. This plot was the cause of the nation's evils: "It is this unnatural infusion of a *system of favoritism* into a government which in a great part of its constitution is popular, that has raised the present ferment in the nation."⁶

Burke's outline of the plot was purposely vague; furthermore, he claimed that he was not attacking any one individual but rather a new "system, which, without directly violating the letter of the law, operates against the spirit of the whole constitution."⁷ Still, an appearance of plausibility in the plot, and the accompanying suspicions which seemed to support it, gave it a particularity and historical credibility. The amplified legend includes some details which Burke did not discuss or only hinted at. The successor to George II was to have been Frederick, Prince of Wales, who had surrounded himself at Carleton House with the king's opponents, one of whom was Lord Bute. As the legend has it, Bute and the princess dowager formed a sordid sexual alliance after Frederick died, and together they educated George to become a patriot king, that is, a king after Bolingbroke's model, who would take control of the nation and lead it himself. His mother's famous charge, "George, be a king!" meant that he was not to be another George II; in short, he was not to lose still more of the royal power and influence which the crown once had. When George III ascended the throne, the legend continues, he plotted to get rid of the ministers, first Pitt, then Newcastle, so that he could replace them with his own; and indeed Newcastle's successor was Lord Bute. Even when Bute left the ministry, however, he was reputed to have secret access to the king, which prevented any other ministry from succeeding. Thus the government policy was determined not so much by the ostensible ministry as by the "closet" ministry of Bute and the king's friends.

A group known as the "king's friends" did in fact exist, but they claimed to be simply patriotic men trying to eliminate corruption and faction by cooperating with the king. Burke put them in a more sinister light, and in this light they were seen by most nineteenth-century historians. What must be understood, however, is that Burke was purposely exaggerating the power of the king's friends in order to combat the real danger of Bolingbroke's program, which could cause a constitutional change. The vague but plausible "plot" of a secret court party was itself a rhetorical device calculated to further Burke's statesmanship, which consisted of making parties based on principles a respectable part of the constitution.[8]

Obviously, such a legend — whether fiction, fact, or some combination of the two — could serve Junius' ends very well indeed, and after Burke's *Thoughts* there are unmistakable appearances of it. Junius hints strongly at a shameful connection "between the Princess Dowager and her favourite the Earl of Bute" and berates their "plan of tutelage and future dominion over the heir apparent" (p. 160 n.). Before the appearance of the *Thoughts* Junius had written vaguely of an unconstitutional "system" in the government, but in May, 1770, in the first letter to appear after Burke's pamphlet, he follows Burke explicitly: "A new system has not only been adopted in fact, but professed upon principle. Ministers are no longer the public servants of the state, but the private domestics of the Sovereign. One particular class of men are permitted to call themselves the King's friends, as if the body of the people were the King's enemies . . . ." Appended to this in the collected edition is a footnote, quoting Davenant, which defines "king's friends" as "an ignorant, mercenary, and servile crew; unanimous in evil, diligent in mischief, variable in principles, constant to flattery, talkers for liberty, but slaves to power." The king, who figures very little in Burke's *Thoughts,* does not escape Junius' onslaught. "Secluded from the world, attached from his infancy to one set of persons, and one set of ideas, he can neither open his heart to new connexions, nor his mind to better information" (pp. 201-2). The "one set of ideas" makes the king's part in the new system much more explicit than it is in Burke's. The implication is that as Prince of Wales he was brainwashed with Bolingbroke's notions of a patriot king, and now he is trying to practice them, at the expense of the English constitution.

Part of the vagueness in Burke's account of the plot lies in his studied avoidance of naming those who concocted the plot. He simply says it was "devised by a certain set of intriguing men.... This project, I have heard, was first conceived by some persons in the court of Frederick Prince of Wales."[9] Burke is also unclear as to who carried out the plot. He only says that Bute is not responsible directly; sometimes it is "his creatures."[10] The same ambiguity, though in different form, is also found in Junius. His specialty being sharp attacks on individuals, it is not like Junius to avoid aiming direct attacks at his enemies. Responsibility for the plot is attached to particular people, but, as if uncertain or perhaps capitalizing on the vagueness of Burke's account, he fixes responsibility on different people. At first, Lord Mansfield, the chief justice is the scapegoat ("I see through your [Mansfield's] whole life, one uniform plan to enlarge the power of the crown, at the expence of the liberty of the subject" (p. 208). By January, 1771, in a Junius letter signed "Domitian," he is propagating the notion that the culprit is, without a doubt, the king's mother:

Her Royal Highness's Scheme of Government, formed long before her Husband's Death, is now accomplished. She has succeeded in disuniting every Party, and dissolving every Connexion; and, by the mere Influence of the Crown, has formed an Administration, such as it is, out of the Refuse of them all.... I consider her not only as the original creating Cause of the shameful and deplorable Condition of this Country, but as a Being whose Operation is uniform and permanent.... Every Office in Government is filled with Men, who are known to be her Creatures, or by mere Cyphers incapable of Resistance. (pp. 482–83)

When Junius wrote notes for the collected edition, however, he laid the blame squarely at Bute's door (p. 160 n.).

In determining Junius' position, one must never forget his rhetoric. Junius' world is filled with devils, and if it serves his purpose, he puts no limit on the number of chief devils. Furthermore, there is one devil whom he is cautious of attacking. In the passage already quoted, Junius explains to Wilkes that he has treated the king with "undeserved moderation" — not Bute, not "even" the princess dowager, but the king himself is chiefly to be blamed and detested. When Junius begins exploring the issue of the king's friends, his attacks on the king become noticeably more vicious. The king is "the basest fellow in the kingdom." "From the moment he ascended the throne, there is no crime, of which human nature is capable ... that has not appeared venial in his sight" (pp. 246–48). Such is Junius' "moderation." But such, too, is Junius', though not Burke's, cause of the present discontents. *"He alone* is the Mark" (p. 430).

It appears, then, that Junius took Burke's legend of the king and king's men with great seriousness. He seems genuinely alarmed about "the secret system of the closet" which has been "invariably pursued, from the moment of his present Majesty's accession" (p. 218). But his alter ego, Philo-Junius, allows the possibility of doubt in a carefully worded passage: "Whether or no there be a *secret system* in the closet, and what may be the object of it, are questions, which can only be determined by appearances, and on which every man must decide for himself" (pp. 226–27). This is presented as rhetorical doubt, and the "proper" response is certain: there does *appear* to be a secret system whose object is to capture unlimited power for the king; therefore it must be so. But by whose "appearances"? Junius', of course. Philo-Junius' rhetorical doubt will not dissuade those who want to believe, but it does serve to warn the critical reader that the truth and the appearance may differ. The existence of such a passage suggests that Junius was not willing to accept the appearance himself, but was willing for his noncritical readers to accept it. Precisely the same ruse is used by Burke to establish his legend as fact for those willing to judge by appearances. "Whether all this," Burke writes, after outlining the plot, "be a vision of a distracted brain, or the invention of a malicious heart, or a real faction in the country, must be judged by the *appearances* which things have worn for eight years past."[11] Burke must be credited for giving the legend its form, but Junius learned his lesson well. Junius' effectiveness after the *Thoughts* depended to a large extent on his ability to portray convincingly the "Sovereign of a free nation" — and that nation, England — "possessed with a design to make himself absolute" (p. 226).

If, as I have argued, Junius did not take the plot literally, why is it a major theme of the *Letters?* The answer is that while the plot was not literally true, it effectively dramatized a truth (to Junius), namely, that the crown was gaining power, especially by dominating Parliament, so as to cause a dangerous imbalance in the constitution. The constitution required a delicate balance of the crown, Parliament, and people, and Junius thought he perceived the balance going awry. The real issue was the amount of influence the crown held over Parliament and the people. The Wilkes episode was an excellent example of the crown and Parliament combining to destroy the rights of the people to freely elect their representatives; hence the apparent conspiracy became Junius' major concern.

In his *Thoughts* Burke contrived a distinction between royal "prerogative" and royal "influence" — prerogative being an old power of the crown based on ancient custom, and influence being a new power, established since the Revolution and originally divided between the king and the Whig ruling families. The danger now is not prerogative, which is "dead and rotten," but influence, for the king's friends want this power for the crown.[12] Junius was as willing to adopt this distinction as he was to adopt Burke's plot — "We have nothing to apprehend from prerogative, but every thing from undue influence" (pp. 230–31) — but he was not comfortable with the distinction. It was merely a change in name: "that pernicious influence, (for which our Kings have wisely exchanged the nugatory name of prerogative)" (p. 283). The danger from the power of the crown was the same, "whether influence or prerogative" (p. 22).

The fact is that Junius had no need for this distinction. Burke had devised it to show the separation between the court party (king's friends) and the ministry. Junius paid lip service to this plot (as in "the secret system of the closet") and was willing that it be believed because it served his cause, but he actually saw no such distinction. For him the king's friends and the ministry were identical. "The ministry," he wrote, "are labouring to draw a line of distinction between the honour of the crown and the rights of the people" (p. 224) and in doing so they are attempting to gain excessive power for the crown. In Burke's legend, the ministry consisted of weak, inept dupes; the court party was the dangerous evil. For Junius, the ministry was inept *and* evil; there was no need to look to a separate court party for the cause of the discontents. Junius' views were shorter than Burke's. His purpose was to destroy the ministry and force a more acceptable one on the king, thereby correcting the imbalance of the constitution; Burke's purpose was to destroy the potential evils of Bolingbroke's ideas of a patriot king by establishing respectable parties based on principle. For his rhetorical purposes Junius found Burke's legend very useful but partly dispensable.

IV   *The Ministry*

The bulk of Junius' political attack, then, was not on the king or a secret court party but on the king's ministers. The burden of the attack fell on the duke of Grafton, the first minister from 1767 until early 1770; indeed, Lecky says that Grafton is "now chiefly remembered as the object of the most savage of all the invectives of Junius."[13] Although Grafton was the unfortunate main object, Junius' attacks covered a wide range of ministers in power during the early years of George III's reign. The *Letters* comprise a detailed textbook, albeit a highly prejudiced one, of the politics of this era.

The first decade of the reign was a period of considerable ministerial instability — Junius mockingly referred to it as a rotation system — and it was Junius' self-appointed task to promote the instability until the right people, such as Grenville or Chatham, were forced upon the king. When George came to the throne in 1760 he retained the existing coalition of Newcastle and Pitt, though against his will, since they represented to him the Whig connections which he wished to eliminate. Whether by calculation or accident, however, he soon managed to eliminate Pitt, who resigned when his desire to pursue war with Spain was ignored, and eventually Newcastle as well. The king was then delighted to ask his tutor and "dearest friend" Bute to form a ministry to pursue a peace policy. The Peace of Paris, negotiated by the duke of Bedford in 1763, was extremely unpopular in England. This, with Bute's Scottish nationality — the object of considerable English prejudice — and his reputation as the dowager's lover and the king's evil influence, made for a sufficiently miserable and, therefore, short ministry. Bute, a suave, witty man, was not cut out to be a first minister. The king's "favorite," as he was popularly called, was replaced by Junius' favorite, George Grenville, a Whig aristocrat and brother-in-law of Pitt. Grenville had a sharp mind for finances but did not have the support of the king. To reduce the national debt, Grenville conceived the ill-fated Stamp Act as a tax on legal documents in the American colonies, but this was met by revolt in America and repealed by the following Rockingham ministry, which, however, declared a *right* to tax the colonies as Grenville wished. Rockingham, aided by Burke, led the shortest ministry of all; the following year (1766) he was replaced by the Great Commoner, Pitt, now the earl of Chatham.

To those who felt the country could be guided only by a "great man," Chatham was the obvious answer. He did not believe in party government but he could bind men together by the force of his personality and strength of his beliefs, and he could convey this sense of unity and purpose to the nation. But by renouncing his seat in Commons, Chatham lost considerable popular support as well as the power that he used to wield in that House. Furthermore, Chatham was seriously ill, both physically and mentally. By March, 1767, he was totally debilitated and had to retire from public life, leaving the control of government to his young first lord of the treasury, Grafton.

Without Chatham's leadership, however, his cabinet was disunified and ineffectual. Grafton was an indolent and reluctant leader; the chancellor, Lord Camden, was spiteful about Chatham's retirement, suggesting to others a disbelief in his illness; and the duke of Bedford's friends — a group whom Chatham most devoutly wished to keep out because of their anti-American views — were invited into the ministry and indeed gained control of it. Chatham, however, was not allowed to withdraw from the ministry; his name, with its potency, lent the ministry a respectability and cohesiveness that in reality it lacked. Though the state or cause of his illness was not fully known, he was near death and probably would have died had it not been for Lady Chatham's ministrations. All visits were denied; the king's letters — pleas that Chatham return — were sent back unread. During this period, Junius sent a letter to Chatham marked "Private and secret: to be opened by Lord Chatham only," intended like the king's letters to urge Chatham to action, but by different arguments. Chatham was being betrayed, Junius argued, by all of his ministers. "During your absence from administration, it is well known that not one of the ministers has either adhered to you with firmness, or supported . . . those principles, on which you engaged in the King's service."Camden, Shelburne, Northington, Conway — all Chatham supporters — were berated, but the chief blame fell on Grafton: "It is understood by the publick that the plan of introducing the Duke of Bedford's Friends entirely belongs to the Duke of Grafton, with the secret concurrence, perhaps of Lord Bute, but certainly without your Lordship's consent, if not absolutely against your Advice" (pp. 443–44).

In October, 1768, Chatham mustered only enough energy to resign, ostensibly because of the dismissal of Amherst as governor of Virginia but actually because the policy of the Grafton ministry had become entirely different from his own. Junius no doubt would have preferred Chatham to return to the ministry in full health to curb the influence of Grafton and Bedford's friends; in his private letter he had professed himself convinced that "if this Country can be saved, it must be saved by Lord Chatham's spirit, by Lord Chatham's abilities." But Chatham would have met opposition in Grafton's ministry and, in addition, he had not recovered from his illness. Thus his withdrawal was acceptable in that it weakened the ministry, giving the opposition hopes for its fall.

When Junius opened his systematic attack on the ministry in January, 1769, he was attacking Grafton's inheritance from Chatham, plus his alliance with the Bedfords, in the midst of the Wilkes crisis. Within a year Chatham had recovered, and from his seat in the House of Lords led the opposition to the ministry. Lord Chancellor Camden, who had not been entirely faithful to his leader during Chatham's illness, now began attacking the ministry — of which he was part — for seating Luttrell in Commons instead of Wilkes. For this defection he was of course dismissed — or, as Junius put it, "tyrannically forced out of his office, not for want of abilities, not for want of integrity, or of attention to his duty, but for delivering his honest opinion in parliament, upon the greatest constitutional question, that has arisen since the revolution" (p. 177). The united opposition, led by Chatham, Rockingham, and Grenville, was eager to take over the power, and Camden's departure, like Granby's shortly thereafter, was calculated to prepare for a change of ministry.

The ministry, meanwhile, to fill the post of chancellor, fixed on Charles Yorke, a member of the Rockingham party. Yorke at first refused to desert his party to join the ministry, though the position had long been his ambition. The king himself tried to persuade him but again he refused. The following day, however, he vacillated, attended the king's levee, was called into a secret conference with the king, and finally was prevailed on to accept the post at the expense of his friends and his principles. The desertion filled Yorke with remorse and the next day he was dead, probably from suicide. This event staggered the ministry; both Grafton and the king were henceforth "murderers" to Junius. A few days later, on January 27, Grafton resigned.

Junius detested both Grafton's person and his policy, so much so that his malice calculated to destroy the ministry is often indistinguishable from his personal ill will. But Grafton was notorious for his neglect of business and his personal misconduct; he thought, as Horace Walpole said, "the world should be postponed to a whore and a horse race."[14] One of his most imprudent actions was to appear at the opera in the presence of the queen with his mistress, Nancy Parsons Horton, known to many as "the Duke of Grafton's Mrs. Horton, the Duke of Dorset's Mrs. Horton, everybody's Mrs. Horton." (She later married a viscount and became Lady Maynard.) This incident and this mistress Junius was fond of recalling for public edification and amusement. In fact, Grafton suffered from an unfortunate marriage, which supplied Junius with more ammunition. As first minister, he was often preoccupied with a complex divorce from his first wife, who was seduced and later married by her paramour, the duke of Bedford's nephew. When the divorce was effected, Grafton dropped his mistress and married the duke of Bedford's niece. This strange "double marriage" was made to order for Junius' satire, especially since he detested Bedford as much as he did Grafton. Junius had no difficulty putting this second marriage to "a near relation of one who had debauched his wife" (p. 76) in an ignoble light. Nor was Grafton's ancestry immune from attack. Descended from the illegitimate son of King Charles II, Grafton had, in Junius' eyes, the tainted blood of a Stuart.

Grafton did not want to be first minister, nor was he particularly fit for it, and to follow Chatham would be difficult for any man. He was very young for the position — "a singular instance of youth without spirit," Junius said — and capriciously made threats to resign. Frequently, he was in London doing the business of the government only one day a week and in the country the rest. Junius' portrait of the minister as a young rake destroying his nation was highly exaggerated but contained enough truth to make itself felt.

Furthermore, Grafton was vulnerable to charges of deserting his friends to the extent of being, in Junius' words, "an apostate by design" (p. 27). Junius charged him with betraying Wilkes, then Chatham. "Lord Chatham formed his last administration upon principles which you [Grafton] certainly concurred in, or you could never have been placed at the head of the treasury. By deserting those principles, and by acting in direct contradiction to them, in which he found you were secretly supported in the closet, you soon forced him to leave you to yourself, and to withdraw his name from an administration, which had been formed on the credit of it" (p. 70). Grafton in cahoots with the king's friends had "forced"

Chatham out! — not a word is mentioned of Chatham's debili-
tating illness. This account is far from the truth, yet by 1768 the
Grafton ministry was clearly pursuing quite different policies than
Chatham would have; thus the charge that Grafton "betrayed"
Chatham's principles had some validity. In defense of Grafton,
however, it could be said that Chatham's cabinet was not formed
on "principles"; rather it was a strange conglomeration of individuals united under the influence of the Great Commoner's personality. Chatham did not propagate a party program such as Burke
recommended, and when he could not actively lead his ministers
there was no cohesive force to unite them. Grafton's "betrayal"
was a crime to Junius primarily because Junius much preferred
Chatham's policies to Grafton's.

The attacks of Junius' letters on Grafton occur in three phases:
first in 1769, the last year of Grafton's ministry; second on Grafton's departure as first minister (Letter XXXVI): and third, on
Grafton's entry in June, 1771, into the North ministry as lord privy
seal (Letters XLIX, L, LVII, and LXVII). Junius' early notices of
the first minister identify him as the leader of governmental ineptitude in the Wilkes affair; they indulge in some personal scurrility,
such as mentioning betrayals and mistresses, but for the most part
they are concerned with Grafton's measures and not the man himself. However, in Letter XII, he changed his tactics. Grafton did
not seem at this point to be losing ground; he had the confidence of
the king, he seemed all too firmly entrenched in his position, and he
had completed his divorce and remarried into the Bedford clan.
Junius therefore attempted to wound him by a frontal attack first
on his private history — betrayals, mistresses, illegitimate ancestors, ignoble marriages — and then on his public conduct with
respect to American policy, Corsica, and domestic policy. The pre-
dominance of personal satire indicates that Junius was determined
to draw a scathing portrait or "character" of Grafton rather than
persuade through argumentation. "I do not give you to posterity,"
he concludes his letter to Grafton, "as a pattern to imitate, but as
an example to deter; and as your conduct comprehends every thing
that a wise or honest minister should avoid, I mean to make you a
negative instruction to your successors for ever" (p. 74).

Junius' immediate aim was to get Grafton out of office to make
way for a more acceptable ministry from the opposition —
Chatham, Grenville, or Rockingham. At the end of 1769 and at the
opening of a new parliamentary session in January, 1770, he

seemed to be on the verge of success: the opposition was stronger due to the recovery of Chatham, and Grafton's troubles were greater, climaxed by the death of Yorke. Hence, the resignation of Grafton on January 28 brought joy — but only briefly. The king turned not to the opposition but to Grafton's chancellor of the exchequer, Lord North, who successfully formed a new ministry. Junius could be expected to turn his attention to North, but he took leave, as he hoped, of Grafton with a letter on his resignation, reviewing his miserable career and trying to crown it by making his departure appear contemptible. Grafton had "disgraced and deserted" the king and brought the nation to "the brink of destruction." "You began with betraying the people, — you conclude with betraying the King" (pp. 179–80). The letter is an admirable specimen of Junius' ability to pile accusation upon innuendo upon insult, all with a meticulously controlled yet bitter scorn. It was intended as the parting blow at Grafton and as a transition to new attacks on the North ministry, which retained many of the same ministers, including the Bedford faction, and would therefore prove no more acceptable to Junius.

North, however, did not receive the same personal and diabolical attention that Grafton had. Junius had noticed and scorned "Lord North's genius for finance" (p. 28) in 1769, and then attacked him occasionally as first minister, but he conceded that North was "perhaps ... no more than the blind, unhappy instrument of Lord Bute and her Royal Highness the Princess of Wales" (p. 206). Instead of transferring his personal invective to North, Junius had occasion to continue it against Grafton, who in June, 1771, accepted the ministerial post of lord privy seal; thus, though the ministry had changed in name, it had from Junius' point of view changed little in fact. A further attack on Grafton had the advantage of impressing his audience with the similarity between the old and new ministers, and, therefore, impressing them with the necessity for a still different ministry formed from the opposition. By virtue of the number and vehemence of the attacks on Grafton, he had become for Junius and his readers almost a symbol of the dishonesty, ineptness, and danger to constitutional freedom in the English government. In a rhetorical sense, Junius had linked his own identity to Grafton's, for he was the minister's antithesis. Where Grafton betrayed people and principles, Junius — as he portrays himself — was consistent; where Grafton acted deviously for personal gain, Junius wrote forthrightly for no gain; and where Grafton undermined the constitution, Junius defended it. Without Grafton and the traits Junius attached to him, there could be no need for the existence of a Junius. What Sporus was to Pope in the *Epistle to Dr. Arbuthnot,* Grafton, "and I, my Lord, who do not esteem you the more for the In the greatest of his last attacks on Grafton, Letter XLIX (June, 1771), Junius explicitly ties their fates together. "You would long since have received your final dismission and reward," he tells Grafton, "and I my Lord, who do not esteem you the more for the high office you possess, would willingly have followed you to your retirement." But retirement, if not for one, could not be the fate of the other. "The king is determined, that our abilities shall not be lost to society. The perpetration and description of new crimes will find employment for us both" — the perpetration by Grafton and the description by Junius (p. 247). This letter ignores North entirely in order to execute a brilliant double attack on Grafton and the king. Grafton cannot be justly termed the "meanest and basest fellow in the kingdom" only because that honor must be reserved for *"his* [that is, the king's] sacred character." With equally savage irony but with more subtlety and effect, Junius reviews Grafton's history to the dishonor of the king. "His Majesty is full of justice, and understands the doctrine of compensations. He remembers with gratitude how soon you had accommodated your morals to the necessity of his service; — how cheerfully you had abandoned the engagements of private friendship, and renounced the most solemn professions to the public. The sacrifice of Lord Chatham was not lost upon him. Even the cowardice and perfidy of deserting him [that is, the king, when Grafton resigned as first minister] may have done you no disservice in his esteem. The instance was painful, but the principle might please" (p. 248). With a remarkable explicitness which is sometimes lacking in the less effective letters, Junius bolsters charges that Grafton is guilty of "breach of trust, robbery, and murder" — the last referring to the unfortunate suicide of Yorke. In a private letter to Woodfall which accompanied the letter to be published, Junius professed himself to be "strangely partial" to Letter XLIX. "It is finished with the utmost Care," he said. "If I find myself mistaken in my judgement of this paper, I positively will never write again" (p. 372). The letter is indeed among his best — and Junius did write again.

One of Junius' most formidable enemies was Lord Mansfield, not technically a minister but very closely tied to governmental policies and, as chief justice of the King's Bench, very important in effecting policies. Mansfield was the Newcastle ministry's leader in Commons until he accepted the chief justiceship in 1756, but for over fifteen years he continued to take an active part in government politics, passing through various administrations. This alliance, coupled with some of Mansfield's court decisions, as in the libel cases, inevitably led Mansfield to be identified as a king's friend and supporter of arbitary power. In Junius' survey of the ministry in Letter I, Mansfield is attacked on this count, with specific reference to John Wilkes, the "victim": "A judge under the influence of government, may be honest enough in the decision of private causes, yet a traitor to the public. When a victim is marked out by the ministry, this judge will offer himself to perform the sacrifice. He will not scruple to prostitute his dignity, and betray the sanctity of his office, whenever an arbitrary point is to be carried for government, or the resentment of a court to be gratified" (p. 32).

Mansfield was highly unpopular among the "patriots," but to Junius especially he started with two strikes against him — he was a lawyer and a Scot. In the preface, Junius announced with pride, "I am no lawyer by profession, nor do I pretend to be more deeply read, than every English gentleman should be in the laws of his country" (p. 13). He especially disdained the legal use of precedents because they tend to obscure principles, and he believed most lawyers to be unexceptionable men ("As a practical profession, the study of the law requires but a moderate portion of abilities"). But his objection to law is basically a moral one: "The indiscriminate defence of right and wrong contracts the understanding, while it corrupts the heart. Subtlety is soon mistaken for wisdom, and impunity for virtue" (p. 323). Unlike the lawyer's, Junius' existence depended upon a moral indignation of the head and the heart. To Wilkes, who was naturally curious about the identity of his mysterious correspondent, Junius would only provide negative information. "Though I use the terms of art, do not injure me so much as to suspect I am a Lawyer." And, he added, half-jesting, "I had as lief be a Scotchman" (p. 423). Mansfield had the misfortune of being a Scotchman, an especialy opprobrious trait in the 1760s when so much hatred fell on the Scot, Lord Bute. The title of Wilkes' periodical, *The North Briton,* was intended to inflame this national prejudice. The prejudice, however, was not without its reasons. In 1745, the last attempt of the Stuarts to recover the English crown, Bonnie Prince Charlie landed in Scotland, amassed all of his support there, and marched toward London to destroy the

Hanoverian reign. The scorn for Scotland was pervasive among Englishmen, many of whom were incensed when George III pointedly called himself a "Briton" instead of an "Englishman" at his coronation. In the preface, Junius ended his discussion of Mansfield with a catalog of traits of all Scots — ' the characteristic prudence, the selfish nationality, the indefatigable smile, the persevering assiduity, the everlasting profession of a discreet and moderate resentment" (p. 21). As a young man Mansfield had discreetly supported the Stuart cause, and this was precisely the kind of skeleton in the closet that Junius gloried in. Mansfield's brother — "dearest brother," Junius says — was in fact the Pretender's confidential secretary. Junius, therefore, did not let the people forget that their chief justice was a "rank Jacobite," and though the House of Lords had cleared him of the charge, Junius confidently asserted that Mansfield "frequently drank the Pretender's health upon his knees" :p. 207 n.).

V   *Foreign Policy*

Junius' victims were the English governmental leaders and his issues were usually the domestic policies of the ministry. So little of Junius' efforts are devoted to foreign policies that it is easy to forget, when reading Junius, that England was a world power during this time and that some of its most controversial issues, rivalling even the Wilkes affair, involved foreign affairs. Junius glances at some of them and even devotes considerable attention to the Falkland Islands affair, but for him foreign policy is little more than a means for furthering his domestic attacks.

The most troublesome issue for England in the 1760s and 1770s was the management of the American colonies, and her failure to meet the challenge is well enough known. Despite the fact that this was an issue of the highest political importance, Junius had relatively little to say about it, and what little he said lacked firmness. Before adopting the name of Junius he wrote to the *Public Advertiser* in 1768: "We find ourselves at last reduced to the dreadful alternative of either making war upon our colonies, or of suffering them to erect themselves into independent states. It is not that I hesitate now upon the choice we are to make. Everything must be hazarded" (Wade, II, 192) — hazarded, that is, to prevent their becoming independent. But this attitude against independence was commonplace in 1768 and serves simply to introduce an attack on the ministers responsible for the "dreadful alternative." In 1776, however, Philip Francis opposed war with America. In a letter to his friend D'Oyly he confessed that he had changed his mind. "There was a time when I could reason as logically and passionately as anybody against the Americans; but since I have been obliged to study the book of wisdom, I have dismissed logic out of my library. The fate of nations must not be tried by forms."[15]

As Junius, he does not so much fluctuate in his opinions on America as avoid opinions. When he refers to America, it is usually as a means to attack someone. Thus Grafton, the "patron of America" (p. 72), is attacked by tracing the inconsistency of his changing positions on America, without confronting the issue itself. The king is attacked on the grounds that he has alienated the affections of the Americans, by way of building up the charge that the king is supported only by Jacobites, Tories, and Scots (p. 167), and the king's reprimand to Americans for their Boston Tea Party is condemned, but Junius never tells us *his* attitude toward the Boston Tea Party. With respect to the Stamp Tax on American documents, its repeal, and the ensuing Declaratory Act which asserted a *right* to tax, Junius criticizes Parliament and the ministry for "an odious, unprofitable exertion of a speculative right." "They have relinquished the revenue, but judiciously taken care to preserve the contention" (p. 200). So Junius appears to sympathize with the Americans because of incompetent English ministers, but he never denies the "speculative right" to tax Americans. In fact, Junius' hero was George Grenville, who instigated the Stamp Act, and Grenville is praised in the early non-Junian letters as the only Englishman who knows how to deal with America (Wade, II, 193). By late 1771 Junius has decided that a tax was "impolitic" but that England positively has a right to tax Americans even without representation because denying the right would jeopardize many parts of the constitution. The right, he asserts, is "never to be *exerted,* nor ever to be *renounced*" (pp. 311, 412). It is possible that Junius' hedging on the American question was not timidity or uncertainty, as Merivale maintains,[16] but rather political prudence. Ascribing prudence to Junius may seem odd, but his reprimand to Wilkes for raising the issue of American representative assemblies should be taken seriously: "I must own I think you had no business to revive a question, which should, & probably would, have lain dormant for ever" (p. 412). Junius seems to feel that the best hope for progress on the American issue was to avoid exacerbation — precisely the opposite of his tactics on English domestic politics.

In only one foreign issue did Junius pursue his more typical politics of exacerbation. In 1770 a serious crisis in English foreign affairs nearly led the country into war with Spain over the relatively insignificant Falkland Islands off the coast of South America. Both England and Spain claimed a right to the islands by discovery and first settlement, but neither claim could be proved. Thinking the islands might be valuable in commerce and war, England established a garrison called Port Egmont in 1765. But its distance from Europe and the slowness of communication meant that any conflict over the islands must be carried on by the local rulers without explicit orders from the English or Spanish ministries. In 1769 the English commander, Captain Hunt, ordered a Spanish schooner away from the island, and the Spanish seized the opportunity of this affront to demand that the entire English colony abandon the island. When a series of protests and counterprotests proved ineffectual, a small but heavily armed Spanish fleet forced the English to capitulate on June 10, 1770. A few shots were fired, but the Spanish force was too clearly superior to inspire a battle. It was not until autumn that news of the English eviction finally reached London.

The English government immediately began rebuilding its navy, which had been reduced to a very weak state, and at the same time began negotiations with Spain. For a while at the end of 1770, popular indignation seemed to make war inevitable. In mid-January, 1771, Junius wrote privately to Woodfall: "Depend upon the Assurance *I* give you that every Man in Administration looks upon War as inevitable" (p. 367). But six days later the English and Spanish ministers reached a settlement: Spain agreed to return the islands to the English but explicitly refused to relinquish their right to the islands. Secretly, the English agreed to abandon the islands in the near future. It was a face-saving settlement for both sides which avoided war but left the question of legitimate ownership unsettled.

The settlement aroused a fury of public outrage; Chatham damned it in Commons and Junius in the *Public Advertiser*. The motives of the opposition, and Junius in particular, are not easily analyzed. They are open to suspicion, since many people stood to make money on the stockmarket in the event of war. "These are the men," in Samuel Johnson's words, "who, without virtue, labour, or hazard, are growing rich as their country is impoverished; they rejoice when obstinacy or ambition adds another year to slaughter and devastation; and laugh from their desks at bravery and science, while they are adding figure to figure, and cipher to cipher, hoping for a new contract from a new armament, and computing the profits of a seige or tempest."[17] Philip Francis lost 500 pounds because the war did not take place, which leads his biographer to suggest that the "outburst of zeal for the national honor on the part of Junius may be partly interpreted as an attempt to back a financial speculation of Francis by *bearing* the stock market."[18] A war might also provide the opportunity to overthrow the ministry — a prospect which would delight Junius. Johnson, a friend of the ministry, described this motive with an unflattering image. "There can be none amongst us to whom this transaction does not seem happily concluded, but those who having fixed their hopes on publick calamities, sat like vultures waiting for a day of carnage." For such people "the real crime of the ministry is, that they have found the means of avoiding their own ruin."[19]

Not all reasons for opposing the settlement were ignoble, however. Many believed that England had the only legitimate claim to the islands. The easy eviction of the English from Port Egmont was humiliating for a people who prided themselves on mastery of the seas. That the captors detained the English ship for twenty days after the surrender by removing her rudder was interpreted by a group of lords as "an unparalleled and most audacious insult . . . to the honour of the British flag."[20] Furthermore, the terms of the settlement appeared to some as dishonorable: the king of Spain disavowed the "violent enterprise" but did not punish the perpetrator, the island was returned to England but Spain's prior claim of right remained unaltered, and no restitution was made to England for the large expenditures involved in the eviction and reinstatement.

However complex Junius' motives for opposing the settlement were, his ostensible reasons were limited to the disgrace, humiliation, and dishonor which it brought to England. Letter XLII, published a week after the settlement, is among Junius' most effective letters, though not his most logical. From Junius' review of the episodes of the affair, his analysis of the king's speech, and his comments on the settlement, the letter moves to an eloquent and powerful climax in the form of a "fable": a disgraced king perceives the treachery that has led him to dishonor, is overwhelmed with shame, and humiliates himself before his wronged

Parliament, merchants, landowners, creditors, and populace. War was Junius' alternative to the real, undeserved humiliation of the English people and to the fictional but deserved humiliation of the English king. The prospect of war was made more attractive to Junius by his mistaken belief that France would probably not support Spain.

The letter, however, is singularly lacking in pragmatic arguments: the key words are "right," "honor," "spirit," and "principle." The importance of the islands, for example, "is not in question." Such was the emotion over the Falkland Islands that when Commons voted on the settlement on February 13, two weeks after Junius' letter, the opposition was, from the government's point of view, uncomfortably large: 157 against, 271 for the settled peace. But Johnson's masterly defense of the government settlement, published in March, sufficiently demolished Junius' position. The ministry was justly pleased with Johnson's lucid account of the history of the islands, his convincing practical arguments supporting a peaceful settlement, his realistic appraisal of Spain's predicament, and his timely, vivid reminder of the horrors of war. Although Johnson singled Junius out as "one of the few writers of this despicable faction whose name does not disgrace the page of an opponent" and attacked him at length, Junius chose not to reply. The choice was no doubt wise: the adversary was too formidable and the issue too feeble. Samuel Johnson had more wit than William Draper, and the Falkland Islands affair had less merit than the Wilkes affair. Junius' venture in foreign affairs was, in the end, unsuccessful.

CHAPTER 5

Freedom of the Press

I *The State of the Press*

THE eighteenth-century British constitution was much admired, both at home and abroad, for its balance of powers which allowed considerable liberty for the individual. Men as different as Johnson, Voltaire, Montesquieu, and Burke praised the mixed mode of British government as a model for emulation. By establishing a balance of power among the people, the parliament, and the crown, Britain avoided the tyranny of the mob, on the one hand, and, on the other, the tyranny of an absolute monarch. What was remarkable about eighteenth-century England, compared especially to its archrival France, was the degree of freedom which each individual possessed. "Nothing is more apt to surprise a foreigner," Hume wrote in 1741, "than the extreme liberty which we enjoy in this country, of communicating whatever we please to the public, and of openly censuring every measure entered into by the king or his ministers."[1] But there was no reason for smugness. Some of the liberty was in fact illegal; it could be eliminated by enforcing the law. And the balance upon which liberty rested was by no means beyond disruption; it faced, indeed, some severe trials throughout the century. Junius was among the foremost of those who tried successfully to defend, solidify, and expand the freedom of the press.

The issue was crucial because it was generally agreed that all political liberty available through the mixed mode of government in England rested on the freedom of the press. The press is, of course, not absolutely free in a twentieth-century democracy, but it was much less free in Junius' time, and we owe the freedom we enjoy to the struggle carried on in the eighteenth century. Hume testified to its importance two decades before Junius wrote:

If the liberty of the press ever be lost, it must be lost at once [and not gradually]. The general laws against sedition and libelling are at present as strong as they possibly can be made. Nothing can impose a further restraint but either the clapping an imprimatur upon the press, or the giving very large discretionary powers to the court to punish whatever displeases them. But these concessions would be such a bare-faced violation of liberty, that they will probably be the last efforts of a despotic government. We may conclude that the liberty of Britain is gone for ever when these attempts shall succeed.[2]

Hume identifies two ways by which the freedom of the press — and the liberty of Britain — could be lost: (1) censorship before publication ("clapping an imprimatur upon the press"), and (2) extensive libel prosecutions after publication. Censorship had ceased in England in 1694, long after Milton's great plea for freedom in the *Areopagitica,* and it was never reimposed on the press, though a stage licensing act was passed in 1737 to control the theater. But when the government wanted to protect itself from criticism, it could and did prosecute writers and printers under libel laws. Junius' concern with the freedom of the press largely focussed on those libel laws, in which he and his printer Woodfall became entangled.

There were also several other ways by which the government could control the press. First, Parliament insisted — with less and less success — that the press could not report its proceedings. This privacy was considered an important part of parliamentary privilege, but as the century progressed, more people were interested in knowing the proceedings of their representatives; printers, therefore, found it profitable to include the information. One publisher in the early eighteenth century published monthly reports of the proceedings and avoided prosecution by taking care that the reports portrayed those in power in a favorable light. Others would publish accounts during a recess, when Parliament could not convene to punish them. *The Gentleman's Magazine,* which Johnson wrote for, and the *London Magazine* employed the ruse that they were reporting the events of an imaginary club or fictional land (Magna Liliput) with slightly disguised names — like Walelop or Sir R——t W——le for Walpole — in order to avoid prosecution. But until 1770 Parliament tried to plug the loopholes to preserve their privileges. Finally, the demands of the people — including Junius — were too strident to be circumvented.

Another method by which the press could be controlled was taxation. The government, having discarded its role as censor, discovered that it could raise revenue and discourage ephemeral press criticism at the same time by means of stamp acts. The first Stamp Act of 1712, with others following later, required the publisher to pay a tax on each newspaper or pamphlet. This had the effect of raising prices on papers, making the trade much less profitable, and ruining about half the newspapers.

Indirectly, taxation led to another form of control. Since the publishing business was less lucrative, publishers were more susceptible to political bribery or subsidization. The newspapers became propaganda sheets, paid for by political factions, with the faction in power having the readiest means of support — and therefore the most influential control. Huge sums were spent by the government on newspapers and one-man journals. One historian reports that "from 1731 to 1742 over £50,000 were paid out by the Walpole government to authors and printers of *Free Britons, Daily Courants, Gazetteers* and such journals," and John Almon in the *Anecdotes of Chatham* estimated that during the first three years of the reign of George III 30,000 pounds were spent on the writing and printing of similar publications.[3]

Thus, even without prior censorship, the government could exercise considerable control over the press by means of subsidization, taxation, restriction of parliamentary reporting, and, above all, libel laws.[4]

II   *Junius on a Free Press*

Absolute freedom is a chimera, though in the modern world we often speak of it as the ultimate desideratum. No one is free, however, to shout "Fire!" in a crowded theater which is not in fact on fire; no one is free to excite the violent overthrow of his government; no one is free to act in certain ways that interfere with the relative freedom of others; no one is free to falsely defame others in print. Anyone can do these things, of course, but always at the risk, sometimes the near certainty, of losing every individual freedom he enjoys except the freedom to think what he likes. And even this freedom is effectively curtailed by the use of capital punishment. The pertinent question about freedom is now and was in the eighteenth century, What are the proper limits of freedom?

People do not usually address themselves directly to this question, however, unless they feel that the limits of freedom are being approached, have been reached, or have been exceeded in their society. Junius never discussed the extreme limits of freedom because he was concerned with things as they are and was convinced that these limits had not nearly been reached. The liberty of the individual was one of Junius' concerns, but he could have no effective concerns at all without the liberty to print his opinions and criticisms in the press for the public to read. Thus, for Junius, the freedom of the press was the first of all freedoms. "Let it be impressed upon your minds," he wrote, "let it be instilled into your children, that the liberty of the press is the *Palladium* of all the civil, political, and religious rights of an Englishman" (pp. 8–9). But this was not simply the prudent formulation of a journalist. Hume, as we have seen, maintained a similar position, and DeLolme, author of *The Constitution of England,* observed that the liberty of the press brought about by the abolition of censorship in 1694 was the keystone to the form of government established by the Glorious Revolution.[5] This liberty was of especial importance in a time of crisis, in which Junius believed himself to be living, when the government was led by corrupt, incompetent men, controlled by secret influences around the crown, and determined to subvert the balance of power held by the people and Parliament. In such a time, Junius said, "the liberty of the press is our only resource" (p. 23).

It would be a mistake, however, to view the eighteenth-century press as the virtuous defender of freedom against a despotic ministry that wished to destroy the freedom. Any ministry or government naturally dislikes the criticism of the press and will — as Americans well know — go to elaborate lengths to suppress the attacks of the press. The ministries of Grafton and North were no exception. But it must be remembered that the newspapers and journals were themselves often little more than propaganda sheets. As Lucyle Werkmeister has shown, the newspapers of the 1770s and 1780s were scandal sheets, plagued by unprecedented corruption. "By 1780 there was hardly a 'paragraph' in the newspaper that was not paid for by someone," and "by 1788 every newspaper was in the pay of one political faction or another."[6] Publishers were businessmen, and not the least of their concerns were surviving and making money.

In Junius' time the newspapers had some measure of independence because of revenue derived from advertising, though they still had political biases. The freedom that Junius wished to defend was the freedom to have differing biases in the press. The ministry was naturally displeased with any criticism but especially with the vehement scurrility and abuse heaped upon it by Junius and other opposition writers. Junius chose not to deny the scurrility but argued that the ministerial writers could and did respond in kind. "Yet if news papers are scurrilous," he publicly addressed Blackstone, "you must confess they are impartial." With each faction able to attack and defend freely, "the scales are equally poised. It is not the printer's fault if the greater weight inclines the balance" (p. 94). This is clearly the argument of the side with the more successful press — and Junius, of course, was largely the cause of the success.

Yet many moderate men were bothered by the fact that the success of the opposition press was achieved through invective and scurrility. Junius was forced to answer the complaint. "It is alledged," he wrote, "that the licentiousness of the press is carried beyond all bounds of decency and truth." But if the characters of private men are defamed, Junius answered, they can and ought to take recourse through the law. In the case of attacks on men in office and their measures, however, Junius asserted that "a considerable latitude must be allowed"; indeed, "a constant examination into the characters and conduct of ministers and magistrates should be equally promoted and encouraged," for such examination places restraints on bad men and impediments in the way of bad measures. Furthermore, when the crown has undue influence over the legislature — which Junius believed to be the case — newspapers can excite "a spirit of resistance . . . among the people" (pp. 14–15). In theory, then, a Grafton or a Mansfield ought to encourage the letters of Junius on the grounds that they arouse the rebellion of the people against bad government and thus serve to promote good government. It is small wonder that the ministry did not look favorably on this argument.

Junius' notion of freedom of the press is clearly of a piece with twentieth-century liberalism. The rights of the individual citizen are asserted and protected; on the one hand, he should be allowed to publish freely his version of truth, and, on the other, he should be legally protected from defamation in the press. The claims of the government and its officials, however, are more limited. Junius does not reject the possibility of the government using libel laws against journalists but says only that "considerable latitude should be allowed"; the more latitude, the better, is the spirit of his argument. And, despite the phrasing of "be allowed," this latitude should not be the result of paternalistic benevolence by the government, but a legal right of the journalist.

This view is widely held today, but Junius wrote when there was substantial rational opposition to it. It is a truism for us, as for Junius, that a free society depends on a free press. Almost everyone in the eighteenth century favored "freedom of the press," but the phrase meant different things to different people. It was entirely possible to believe in freedom of the press and at the same time believe that a man had no right to publish criticism of the government. To Junius' archenemy, Lord Mansfield, the phrase meant simply the absence of censorship. In the Woodfall trial Mansfield instructed the jury "that the liberty of the press consisted in every man having the power to publish his sentiments without first applying for a licence to anyone; but if any man published what was against the law, he did it at his peril, and was answerable for it in the same manner as he who suffers his hand to commit an assault, or his tongue to utter blasphemy" (Wade, I, 472). But this depends on what is "against the law," and Mansfield included considerably more in that category than Junius found compatible with freedom. Obviously, with very strict laws and the necessary enforcement, such an arrangement could be as repressive as prior censorship.

Yet Mansfield's was by no means an extreme position. Samuel Johnson had a powerful commitment to individual liberty: he once scandalized a group of dignitaries by proposing a toast to another rebellion of West Indian slaves, and he mocked the American patriots for writing about independence at the same time that they owned slaves. But Johnson was not convinced that punishment after publication was preferable to censorship before publication. His opinion, in its practical effect, is strikingly confirmed by twentieth-century obscenity trials: "This punishment, though it may crush the author, promotes the book; and it seems not more reasonable to leave the right of printing unrestrained, because writers may be afterwards censured, than it would be to sleep with doors unbolted, because by our laws we can hang a thief." He disagreed with Milton's plea for "unbounded freedom" in the *Areopagitica* because such freedom involved dangers no less frightening than those of censorship. This is the dilemma: "If nothing may be published but what civil authority shall have previously approved, power must always be the standard of truth;

if every dreamer of innovations may propagate his projects, there can be no settlement; if every murmurer at government may diffuse discontent, there can be no peace; and if every skeptick in theology may teach his follies, there can be no religion.'' Milton's (and Junius') understanding of freedom of the press, in Johnson's view, led to "no settlement," "no peace," and "no religion."

Junius had no sense of this dilemma because he was more concerned with liberty than with stability. Johnson scoffed at the abstraction, "liberty," as the cant slogan of self-interested politicians like Wilkes. "The notion of liberty," he said, "amuses the people of England, and helps keep off the *taedium vitae*. When a butcher tells you that *his heart bleeds for his country,* he has, in fact, no uneasy feeling.''[7] The people are better served, in Johnson's view, by a stable monarchy, and one source of stability is the limiting of "licentious" writings — those which publish opinions pernicious to society. The people, by giving up certain freedoms to the government, gain in return the freedom to live in a civilized, orderly society which is powerful enough to protect its citizens from outside aggression. Unlimited freedom of the press would lead, Johnson feared, to anarchy — the opposite of what a government is expected to provide. Therefore, the individual may think whatever he pleases; he has complete freedom of conscience. But he may not publish whatever has a tendency to disrupt the government or society. "A man may be allowed to keep poisons in his closets," in Swift's words, "but not vend them about as cordials."

The debate about freedom of the press in the eighteenth century was essentially a debate over the degree to which that freedom should be limited. Both Johnson and Junius agreed that there must be limits, but they disagreed where. Junius admittedly wished to arouse a "spirit of resistance" among the people by means of the press, whereas Johnson felt that such resistance was inimical to government and genuine liberty. The issue was a large one; it was fought during Junius' time; and the victor was the modern, liberal notion of freedom of the press.

III   *The Libel Trials*

The stage for the struggle to gain a more liberal definition of freedom of the press was first the law courts, and later Parliament.

The most effective method the government had for controlling the press was the law of libel. It was based on the following tenets: publication of seditious libel was a crime; publication of such material, which included writing, selling, or distributing, as well as printing, was in itself a criminal act regardless of intention; the truth of the allegations was immaterial; and the jury was permitted to determine only the fact of publication, not whether the publication was libellous.[8] The definition of seditious libel was broad enough to cover anything from false and malicious attacks on the government to criticism of it or even simple disrespect. Anything which tended to cause a breach of peace was subject to prosecution, and this was vague enough to allow innumerable possibilities.

The theory behind the libel law was simply that all governments, in order to function, need the confidence of the citizens. Anyone who engages in political criticism undermines that confidence and hence the effectiveness of the government. For a government to rule best, it is obliged to stifle views which tend to hinder the implementation of its policies. If this tendency were decided by a jury of citizens, however, the laws might be liberally interpreted. But in England, the government itself through its appointed judges, decided which publications were seditious and which not. The juries were allowed to determine only "matters of fact," that is, whether the publication was in fact published by the person charged. "Matters of law," including whether the publication was indeed seditious, were left entirely to the judge. Obviously, in many cases the juries were virtually useless. The fight for greater freedom of the press, then, became a fight for the increased rights of juries, and Junius' printers found themselves in the middle of the struggle.

Many works critical of the government were published without being prosecuted, allowing the press considerable freedom in actual fact, but the government could nonetheless determine libel without appealing to a jury. In 1752 a bookseller named William Owen was tried for publishing a critical pamphlet. He had, indeed, published it, which was all the jury was to decide, but his defense, Charles Pratt, later Lord Camden and chancellor of England, urged the jury to return a not guilty verdict on the grounds that the substance of the pamphlet was not "seditious, malicious, wicked, criminal and false." Libel, he argued, must be determined by the publisher's intention, and this was a matter of "fact" not "law." The practice of the common law, however, was to limit the role of the jury, and the chief justice accordingly instructed the jury to determine only the fact of publication. Their verdict of not guilty was a clear defiance of the bench. In the next two decades more juries of libel cases rebelled by refusing to follow the instructions of the bench. It became very difficult for the government to prosecute libel cases successfully.

On December 19, 1769, Woodfall published Junius' notorious Letter XXXV, the "Address to the King," which audaciously advised the king, attacked his policies, and even threatened deposition. It was Junius' most daring, pungent, and widely read letter. Other newspapers reprinted it immediately and the government acted swiftly to punish it. Because they were ignorant of Junius' identity, the government decided to prosecute his publishers. Within two days of the appearance of the letter the attorney general, DeGrey, acted by information, that is, without a grand jury, filing charges against Woodfall of the *Public Advertiser,* John Almon of the *London Museum,* John Miller of the *London Evening Post,* Henry Baldwin of the *St. James's Chronicle,* and two other publishers of the letter. In private letters to his publisher, Junius urged him to "stand firm — (I mean with all humble appearances of Contrition)" and tried to reassure him that "no Jury, especially in these times" would allow him to be punished. He also promised to pay the expenses that Woodfall incurred in the trial (pp. 360–62).

The first publisher to be tried, however, was not Woodfall but Almon. This was odd, since Almon's paper had only reprinted the letter, and indeed that was done without Almon's knowledge, since he was out of town. When he found out, he ordered the publication to be ceased. But Almon had been offensive to the government on previous occasions and, more important, his trial could be held in Westminster, where the juries were notably less rebellious than those in London. With a favorable decision in the first trial, the government would stand a far better chance of winning the other trials. Therefore, on June 2, 1770, Almon was tried in the Court of the King's Bench with Lord Chief Justice Mansfield presiding. He was charged with having "by such wicked, artful, scandalous, and malicious allusions, suppositions, and insinuations... most unlawfully, wickedly and maliciously aspersed, scandalized and vilified our said present sovereign Lord the King."[9] Sergeant Glynn, Wilkes' friend, ably handled the defense, but upon being instructed to determine the fact of publication only, the jury returned a verdict of guilty. Given Almon's extenuating circumstances which did not apply to the other publishers, the government seemed to be in a position to win easy victories in the other trials.

Woodfall's trial took place on June 13 with Mansfield again presiding, but this time in Guildhall in the City of London. In the defense, Glynn followed Camden's argument that intention and libel were "matters of fact" and made a strong emotional appeal to the jury. Mansfield had the law on his side, however, and the jury was so instructed. After deliberating for ten hours, their unorthodox verdict was: "Guilty of printing and publishing only." What this meant, however, was not clear. Mansfield asserted that since the jury was limited to deciding on publication, of which Woodfall had been found guilty, he was himself free to determine the libel and sentence Woodfall accordingly. Glynn, however, argued that the jury's "only" expressly prohibited this: his client, in short, was vindicated. Mansfield postponed his decision to the next session.

The jury's verdict boded an ill wind for the government. When Miller and Baldwin were tried on July 18 at Guildhall, the two juries independently reached decisions of not guilty. The London populace was overjoyed. A crowd gathered outside Mansfield's house on Bloomsbury Square and gloated over the humiliation of the government. Burke, no friend of the ministry, was technically correct when he asserted in Parliament that "the law is beaten down, and trampled upon." The victory of the publishers was in fact a defeat for law, since the juries were consciously flouting the established law. But there was a common sense in the judgment of the juries. Their notion of libel differed greatly from the government's, and their rebellion against the legal charge was one way of making the government more responsive to the opinions of the populace. One member of a libel jury later became publisher of the prestigious *Times*. His account reflects the spirit of the decisions: "I was one of the jury who tried Junius' letters to the king. ... The printer of the *St. James's Evening* was acquitted as the jury did not choose to vest a power in the Court to give a sentence ... of having wilfully, maliciously and seditiously published the papers when only the mere sale in the common course of his business was proved."[10]

Almon's verdict of guilty stood, of course, and he received a stiff fine for publishing Junius' letter. But Woodfall's ambiguous verdict was never resolved. When he appeared for his retrial, the prosecution confessed that it had lost its evidence; its copy of the December 19 *Public Advertiser* was nowhere to be found. Whether this was the truth or merely a government ruse to extricate itself from the unsuccessful proceedings never became clear, but Woodfall was free, with only the considerable expense of his trial to pay. The other publishers who had been charged were quietly forgotten.

IV   *Parliamentary Opposition*

The London juries were not alone in opposing the ministry's libel prosecutions. Junius fulminated against Mansfield, and Parliament convened for its winter session on November 13, after the four trials but before the sentencing of Almon or the resolution of Woodfall's case. Both Junius and the opposition in Parliament attacked Mansfield and the ministry for its use of the libel law. Junius, as usual, was the most vehement. "We have got the Rascal [Mansfield] down," he wrote privately to Woodfall; "let us strangle him if it be possible." "I will never rest 'till I have destroyed or expelled that Wretch" (p. 365).

The day after Parliament convened, Junius published a lengthy attack on Mansfield which he hoped would supply the opposition with ammunition against the chief justice. Part of the letter is an attempt to prove that Mansfield's handling of the libel trials was inconsistent and illegal. Although the letter was a highly personal attack, it was more truly an attack on the English libel law. Junius rightly observed that "in other criminal prosecutions, the malice of the design is confessedly as much the subject of consideration to a jury, as the certainty of the fact" (p. 211). If a man's motives have to be considered in a murder trial, and all other criminal cases, it is admittedly difficult to understand why they should not be considered in a libel case. And, as Junius pointed out with perfect clarity, the best judge of what is seditious and what is not is the people themselves, the jury. "The truth is, that if a paper, supposed to be a libel upon government, be so obscurely worded, that twelve common men cannot possibly see the seditious meaning and tendency of it, it is in effect no libel. It cannot inflame the minds of the people, nor alienate their affections from government . . ." (p. 19).

At the beginning of the session, the opposition seemed unusually united, but as the debate wore on, it became clear that there were many divisions within the opposition. The ministry survived the onslaught largely by keeping silent and allowing the opposition to debate itself. In Commons, Glynn unsuccessfully attempted to promote an inquiry into the administration of justice regarding the press. In the House of Lords, Chatham and Camden led the fight against Mansfield. On December 10, Chatham asserted that Mansfield's conduct in the Woodfall trial was "irregular, extrajudicial, unprecedented." The argument had come from Philip Francis, who had written a paper on Mansfield's misconduct, communicated it to Chatham through their mutual friend Calcraft, and heard its phrases and arguments in Chatham's mouth within days. In the *Public Advertiser,* a pro-Mansfield writer attacked but misunderstood the argument, and was corrected by "Phalaris" — probably Francis himself — who quoted Chatham's (and his own) words. Later Junius quoted the speech in the preface to his *Letters,* and assured his readers that the words were "taken with exactness." In all likelihood, they were written for Chatham, reported, then quoted by Junius, that is Francis, himself.[11] The next day, Camden directly challenged Mansfield's conduct of the Woodfall trial by insisting on answers to six legal questions. "I am ready to enter into the debate whenever the noble Lord will fix a day for it." But the chief justice would not debate.

By March, 1771, the opposition had formulated a bill to change the libel law but there was no chance of its passage. The "enacting" bill of Dowdeswell would enact, as an innovation, that juries — not judges — would have a right to determine libel. But the Chathamites refused to support it. They preferred a much stronger "declaratory" bill, which would declare that the law always had allowed the juries this right. Such a bill would not only have determined future policy but would also have rebuked Mansfield and all other judges who had maintained the opposite. The bill did not even come to a vote in 1771.

Not until 1792 did Camden, now an old man of seventy-eight, Thomas Erskine, and Charles James Fox combine to push Fox's Libel Bill through Parliament. The "Act to Remove Doubts respecting the Functions of Juries in Cases of Libel" was finally passed, after decades of agitation, establishing that "the jury is, in regard to libels, to judge of law as well as of fact, of intention as well as of the exterior act." Furthermore, Fox's bill was declaratory, asserting that the version of law that Camden, Junius, Chatham, and Fox had fought for had always been the true one. No doubt this was more a political than a legal judgment, but popular opinion and Junius had clearly been vindicated. Fox's Libel Bill of 1792, and the steps which led to it, constitute an important enlargement of freedom of the press.

V   *The Press in Parliament*

One further press freedom that Junius fought for was the elimination of parliamentary privilege in keeping debates secret. As we have seen, such debates were published from reports by Samuel Johnson, Philip Francis, and many others, but Parliament was always watchful of its prerogative. Although it could sometimes be circumvented, the privilege was noxious to journalists and those who wanted to increase popular influence on the government.

There was considerable friction over this point throughout the eighteenth century, but the crisis came in February, March, and April of 1771. At the instigation of Colonel Onslow, Parliament ordered several offending publishers to appear in the House. Those who did so were pardoned with relative ease. But Thompson of the *Gazetteer,* Wheble of the *Middlesex Journal,* and Miller of the *London Evening Post* refused to respond to the summons. Wilkes had planned a strategy with them which would pit the radicals of the City of London against Parliament. When the publishers refused repeated summonses, they were cited for contempt, and proclamation for their arrest was issued with a 50 pound reward. This was precisely what the London radicals wished. Both Wheble and Thompson allowed themselves to be arrested by their own workmen and carried before Aldermen Wilkes and Oliver and Lord Mayor Crosby, who promptly discharged them and gave the captors a certificate for the reward — which they never received. The House sent its own messenger for the third publisher, but just as he was about to arrest Miller, the messenger was himself arrested and imprisoned for "assaulting and unlawfully imprisoning" a city printer.

The House of Commons was outraged at this breach of privilege and was determined to punish the miscreants. Wilkes, Oliver, and Crosby were summoned to Parliament. Wilkes refused, insisting that he be invited as a member rather than alderman, but the other two officials appeared in all defiance and were promptly imprisoned in the Tower of London. It "resembled the dark Business of a Spanish Inquisition," Junius wrote (p. 493). The London mob were even more defiant than their mayor and alderman: they escorted the captives to the Tower as heroes and forced the members of Parliament to run a gauntlet, nearly killing Lord North. Parliament had a tiger by the tail and was not sure what to do. The question remained, What should be done about

Miller and Wilkes? A committee, after debating a month, concluded that Miller should be arrested. Parliament adopted the report and promptly dropped the matter. The committee had not considered the nice problem of *how* to arrest him, and Parliament had no intention of trying. The rebel Wilkes was punished with equal ingenuity. The House ordered him to appear for examination on April 8 and adjourned itself until April 9. Thus a principle was maintained and an unwanted confrontation avoided, though at the loss of some dignity. Crosby and Oliver remained in the Tower, well provided by their London friends, until Parliament adjourned.

Junius' stand on these events was predictable: he supported Wilkes and the printers and strongly objected to the actions of Parliament. His two letters on the situation (Letter XLIV and another signed "A Whig") were both published in April, when the city officials were in the Tower. He argued that Parliament had "no legal authority to imprison any man for any supposed violation of privilege whatsoever" (p. 233). The Junius letter is not one of his most forceful productions; it is rather one of his labored legal arguments which, as a nonlawyer, did not come easily. "The pains I took with that paper upon privilege," he told Wilkes, "were greater than I can express to you" (p. 421). Junius was especially alarmed at the assertion of privilege, because he believed Parliament was not independent but under the evil influence of the crown, or the "king's men." If parliamentary secrecy and the right to imprison people were allowed to stand, Junius feared the upsetting of the constitution. Furthermore, he believed in the right of the people — including himself — to know what debates and actions took place inside Parliament.

Junius' role in this matter was much less important than his role in the libel trials; Wilkes was largely in command of this battle. But when the smoke cleared, it was evident that the development of freedom of the press had moved forward. Parliament did not withdraw the privilege of secrecy from the record, but they were much less inclined to enforce it after the events of 1771. The publishing of debates became thoroughly acceptable, and when members complained, it was about misrepresentation rather than reporting itself. Thus the press had gained tacit permission to record the procedures of Parliament, and this tended to solidify one of Junius' fundamental tenets: that Parliament was responsible to the people.

CHAPTER 6

The English Constitution

JUNIUS' rhetorical techniques, which are calculated for the most effective attack on the government, often disguise his most fundamental beliefs. He sometimes nearly appears to be a firebrand revolutionary, or as Samuel Johnson said, "a meteor formed by the vapours of putrefying democracy."[1] Looking back at him from our perspective, through the French and American Revolutions and the establishment of democracy in the West, it is tempting to see Junius as the precursor of this form of government. Modern critics speak of his "radical, republican spirit," and one bibliographer has even suggested that colonial and English support for the American Revolution might not have developed without Junius' writings! Junius may seem to exude republicanism and revolution, but such epithets are far from the truth. When one pierces through the calculated satire and rhetoric of Junius, he discovers what may come as a surprise: Junius is a firm, even ardent, supporter of the English constitution. It is, he says, "the noblest monument that human policy has erected" (p. 284). The energy of Junius' attacks derives from his conviction that the "Constitution has been grossly & deliberately violated" (p. 431). Junius saw himself as a conservative, in the root sense of the word: he believed in the existing constitution and wanted above all to maintain its integrity against those who were undermining it.

I The Crown

When Junius published his collected letters, he asserted in his "Dedication to the English Nation" that "when Kings and Ministers are forgotten, when the force and direction of personal satyr is no longer understood, and when measures are only felt in their remotest consequences, this book will, I believe, be found to contain principles, worthy to be transmitted to posterity" (p. 7). The principles he refers to were, however, by no means original with him; they were the constitutional principles established by the revolutionary settlement of 1689, and conservatively interpreted by Junius. The Glorious Revolution was in no way an attempt to overthrow one form of government for another. Rather, it was intended to preserve on a sounder basis the traditional English monarchy, which had been sorely tried in the seventeenth century, first by the republican Cromwell and then by the headstrong Catholic king, James II.

When James culminated his blundering administration by fleeing to France, a parliamentary convention, declaring that he had abdicated the throne, invited William of Orange and his wife Mary (James' daughter) to rule as king and queen. Thus the Protestant crown was restored, but on a significantly different footing: the basis of royal authority was no longer divine right but a title conferred by Parliament. What had been a long rivalry between the crown and Parliament yielded to cooperation, with Parliament taking the upper hand. The legal settlement, and the crucial application of it worked out over the next few decades, made clear that the legislative branch was sovereign; it had established its power to alter the succession or depose a ruler who tried to outstrip his constitutional bounds. The king, still a powerful, influential figure, as well as the chief executive in government, was henceforth essentially the servant of the nation.

There can be no doubt that the crown declined in power and prestige as a result of the revolution, though it was far from approaching the relative weakness of the crown in the twentieth century. Parliamentary control over royal succession was solidified by the Act of Settlement in 1701, which bypassed many candidates in a more direct line of succession in favor of the German house of Hanover. Furthermore, Parliament held an effective check on the crown through its control of the finances. The king still had the prerogative to summon and dismiss Parliament, but this prerogative lost nearly all of its meaning after the revolution since the king was dependent on Parliament for money. As a result, Parliament met every year to supply money and, equally important, to determine its use. The king, however, in the time of Junius, still had considerable financial power because of a lifetime appropriation to be used on personal expenses and on the civil list, for pensions to favorites or politicians whom he wanted to influence, or for parliamentary elections. The king also retained considerable power in foreign affairs. Although the Declaration of Rights prohibited the king from maintaining a standing army in time of peace, he did have the right to raise an army and control it during war. And, as it happened, William III, from Holland, and the early Hanovers, from the German electorate, knew considerably more about European affairs than Englishmen and so took the lead in determining foreign policy. Finally, the king had considerable power to choose his own ministers. The crown, then, after the revolutionary settlement, was the true executive of the government, rather more like the American presidency than the English crown today.

Englishmen of the eighteenth century were justly proud of their "mixed constitution," as opposed to a simple constitution of absolute monarchy or pure democracy. It insured a combination of stability and individual liberty that was not to be equaled elsewhere, and the events of the French Revolution in the 1790s gave Englishmen additional cause for self-congratulation. But few Englishmen could explain the genius of their mixed constitution; this was left to the greater perspective of Frenchmen like Junius' favorite theoretician, DeLolme, and his predecessor, Montesquieu. On matters of theory, Junius defers to DeLolme, "whose essay on the English constitution I beg leave to recommend to the public, as a performance, deep, solid and ingenious" (p. 24).

One of the reasons for the success of England's mixed constitution, according to DeLolme, is the unity of the executive branch. Since all executive power is concentrated in the hands of one person, the source of all executive evils is clear and can more easily be remedied than if the power were shared. But the office itself, though it could be misused, carries with it a certain greatness and awesomeness which serves as a check on the ambition of others in the kingdom. English liberty, in DeLolme's view, exists because of the near impossibility of ambitious men gaining control of the executive branch. But the actual power of the king is simply "the countenancing and supporting with its strength, the execution of the laws." He is not to encroach on the legislative branch, except in certain prescribed ways (as with the royal veto), or on the judicial branch.

That the constitution rested on a delicate balance of its parts, no one in the eighteenth century would deny, but the nature of that balance was open to dispute. George III believed it was his constitutional duty to protect the prerogative of the crown from encroachment by Parliament, but in 1780 Parliament declared that "the power of the crown has increased, is increasing, and ought to be diminished." Junius, of course, not only detested George III as a human being, but feared that he was destroying the balance of powers by controlling Commons. Worse yet, Commons was accepting this control: "they have thrown their whole Weight into the same Scale with the Crown, and ... their Privileges, instead of forming a Barrier against the Encroachments of the other Branches of the Legislature, are made subservient to the Views of the Sovereign ..." (p. 490). Both branches of government were guilty of endangering the constitution.

Junius, unlike DeLolme, never defines the exact nature of the crown's prerogative because in his view the danger lay elsewhere. But in urging Commons to assert its independence, he tends to minimize the importance of the crown itself. Often, Junius seems to view the crown in a way more appropriate to the twentieth than the eighteenth century: "Acts of grace and indulgence are wisely appropriated to [the king], and should constantly be performed by himself. He never should appear but in an amiable light to his subjects." He should have the "heartfelt affections of the populace." Junius speaks much of "the dignity of the crown," of the king's "honour" and "sacred character." The actual executive function Junius assigns elsewhere: "the ministers of the crown are alone responsible for the conduct of public affairs." The sovereign, as a symbol, "represents the majesty of the state"; the ministers execute its business. Only "as the last resource of government" should the king interpose in political affairs (pp. 188–92). Basil Williams' comment on the constitutional situation accurately reflects Junius' view: "The saying, 'The King can do no wrong' signified to the Stuart kings that they were above the law; with the development of the Revolution theory it had come by 1714 to mean that the king in his official capacity could do nothing at all except on the responsibility of ministers holding the confidence of parliament and particularly of the house of commons."[2]

Junius did not deny that the crown was the source of executive power, but he believed that the actual power should be in the hands of ministers responsive to Commons. On the other hand, if the ministers proved to be unresponsive or incompetent, Junius held the king responsible for their replacement. Furthermore, as Junius said in his noble (and insulting) "Address to the King," "It is your interest, as well as your duty to prevent one of the three estates from encroaching upon the province of the other two, or assuming the authority of them all" (p. 171). Ideally, then, the crown is a benevolent symbol which, in time of crisis, ought to wield the actual power of the executive.

II   *The Parliament*

DeLolme's second reason for the success of the English constitution is the division of the legislature into two parts, Lords and Commons, with each part serving as a check on the other. Besides providing general stability, this scheme makes it less likely that the legislature, which has more power than the executive or judiciary, will alter the constitution. Junius has very little to say about the House of Lords as such, though of course he attacks individual peers. But by Junius' time, the Lords were generally considered the inferior house, as they are today. They had no voice in money bills, except to accept or reject them; they could not initiate or alter. They tended also to be dependent on the ministry. The twenty-six bishops voted conservatively, usually with the ministry, as did the sixteen Scottish peers, whose election was controlled by the ministry. Furthermore, many had places close to the king, and others hoped for positions or preferments from the ministry.

Junius' interest centered on the more powerful Commons. Historically, the House of Commons, as the more independent House, was considered the crucial check on the crown, but it was also gaining importance as the body which represented the people of the nation. In the eighteenth century, Commons was hardly representative as we understand the term today. A very small percentage of the population was franchised, and the representation was very unevenly proportioned. In 1774 there were 513 members, fifty-six of whom had constituencies of three or less! Some boroughs were advertised for sale; others were awarded to favorites by wealthy patrons. The county of Middlesex, which included both London and Westminster, sent eight members, while the relatively unpopulated Cornwall sent forty-four.[3] The members themselves were not typical commoners but, as Pitt said, "a parcel of younger brothers" — brothers, that is, of titled noblemen. But the inequities in representation were not considered serious by most people since, as Burke eloquently argued in his "Speech to the Electors at Bristol," each member had a duty to represent the whole of England, not just the borough by which he was elected.

Junius believed that the function of Commons was to represent the people, that is, the nation as a whole. "The constitutional duties of a house of commons, are not very complicated nor mysterious," he wrote. "They are to propose or assent to wholesome laws for the benefit of the nation. They are to grant the necessary aids to the king; — petition for the redress of grievances, and prosecute treason or high crimes against the state" (p. 233). The House consists of "Five Hundred of [the people's] Equals" who are "only interpreters" for the people (pp. 494, 193). This is what alarmed Junius about the Wilkes episode, which has already been discussed: Commons was following not the will of the people but the will of the crown. "The house of commons undoubtedly consider their duty to the crown as paramont to all other obligations" (p. 165) — precisely the wrong sense of duty, in Junius' view, since it strengthened the arbitrary power of the king and denied the electors the right to choose a member by majority vote. The legislature is indeed supreme, he believed, but is limited by law and morality, and does not have the power to destroy liberty. "When we say that the legislature is *supreme,* we mean that it is the highest power known to the constitution: — that it is the highest in comparison with the other subordinate powers established by the laws. In this sense, the word *supreme* is relative, not absolute. The power of the legislature is limited, not only by the general rules of natural justice, and the welfare of the community, but by the forms and principles of our particular constitution" (p. 9). The arbitrary actions of the legislature, prompted by the king's hatred of Wilkes, led to the greatest constitutional crisis of Junius' time.

There was some agitation at the time, especially by a group known as the Supporters of the Bill of Rights — Wilkes' backers — against the existing system of septennial parliaments. The Supporters favored having parliamentary elections annually instead of every seven years. Junius was also wholeheartedly opposed to the system on the ground that long parliaments invited corruption: "The influence of the crown naturally makes a septennial parliament dependent" (p. 238). Indeed, Junius' perception of the importance of separation of powers led him to rank shortened parliaments as the *sine qua non* of improved government. But he believed that stability and experience were necessary to support the cause of the people against the influence of the crown; therefore, he favored triennial elections.

Despite his words about Commons representing the people,

Junius did not feel any democratic zeal for reform such as that which motivated Wilkes' backers to declare that any member of Commons whom they would support should "promote, to the utmost of [their] power, a full and equal representation of the people in parliament." Junius found this plank distinctly distasteful. He would not have rotten boroughs eliminated; he would "not give Representatives to those great trading Towns, which have none at present. — If the Merchant & the Manufacturer must be *really* represented, let them become freeholders by their Industry, and let the Representation of the County be increased" (p. 411). A look at Junius' nondemocratic attitude toward the people and at his sense of political prudence will clarify this paradox of nonrepresentative representatives.

III   *The People*

DeLolme's final reason for the success of the constitution was that the power to initiate legislation is in the hands of the people — by which he meant the House of Commons; thus the liberty of the people, that is, the populace, is protected. Theoretically, these two senses of "people" are united: the Commons represents all commoners. Junius was well aware that this was not literally true, but he was not much bothered by the discrepancy in actual representation. What did bother Junius, as we have seen, is Commons attaching itself to the interests of the crown as opposed to the interests of the people. In such an event, liberty is endangered, and the people have four means of redress: (1) election of other representatives, which should, however, be possible more often than it is, (2) trial by a jury of their peers, (3) petitions of grievances, and (4) resistance or revolution.

If the constitution worked properly, as it usually did, there would be no need for these recourses. It should be absurd to speak of the people contending with Commons, for that would mean "contending with ourselves" (p. 490). But in the turmoils of the late 1760s and early 1770s, such contention was necessary, Junius believed, since Parliament was exceeding its legal bounds. He therefore favored the use of petitions, such as those the City of London presented to the king. "I am far from condemning the late Addresses to the Throne," he wrote to Wilkes. "They ought to be incessantly repeated. The people, by the singular Situation of their Affairs, are compelled to do the Duty of the House of Commons"

(p. 408). When Commons rejects a member elected by the majority of constituents (as in the Wilkes episode), it has rejected "the only criterion, by which our laws judge the sense of the people" and has therefore "essentially altered the original constitution of the house of commons" (p. 171). Hence the necessity of petitions as an alternative means of expressing the sense of the people.

Normally, however, the populace should not be engaged in politics or government at all; they should simply obey the laws legislated by Parliament and executed by the king. The people's obedience should be "voluntary, chearful, and I might also say unlimited" (p. 25). But there is a point at which the people's patience and goodwill give out. "The power of King, Lords, and Commons is not an arbitrary power. They are the trustees, not the owners of the estate. The fee-simple is in *US*" (p. 9). The people have sufficient "understanding" and "spirit" to perceive and act on arbitrary power in their trustees. Junius' letters are filled with dark threats about the consequences of arbitrary power. He reminds the king that what "was acquired by one revolution, . . . may be lost by another" (p. 173), and he warns Parliament that the people's "speech is rude, but intelligible; — their gestures fierce, but full of explanation. Perplexed by sophistries, their honest eloquence rises into action. Their first appeal was to the integrity of their representatives: — the second to the King's justice; — the last argument of the people, whenever they have recourse to it, will carry more perhaps than persuasion to parliament, or supplication to the throne" (p. 193).

The terms describing the people in this threat are revealing — "rude," "fierce," "perplexed," "honest." It was far from Junius' mind that the people should have direct political power in the established government. Indeed, he advised Wilkes — the people's favorite — against such close connection with "the mob": "I would not make myself cheap, by walking the Streets so much as you do" (p. 426). The people's true political function was to serve as a control on the king and Commons. The people are sovereign; it is, after all, their life, liberty, and property which the government is charged with preserving; and they *feel* impingements on life, liberty, and property. But it is the House of Commons which must refine the people's speculations and translate their feelings into political action. Junius invoked the specters of "resistance" and "revolution" but, apart from petitions, he did not explain when and how these were to occur. He does, however, refer the curious reader to the "most ingenious foreigner," DeLolme. The truth is that as long as the freedom of the press was maintained — and the juries were seeing that it was — Junius did not believe that active political resistance or revolution should occur. The effect, Junius believed, would be demagoguery or general destruction; the opposite of the stable, liberal state Junius desired. As DeLolme explains, "The only share [the people] can have in a government, with advantage to themselves, is not to interfere, but to influence — to be able to act, and not to act. The power of the people is not when they strike, but when they keep in awe: it is when they can overthrow everything, that they never need to move."[4]

This, then, is Junius' position: the people have no right to resist, or advantage in resisting, so long as a duly constituted government is functioning. It would have been foolish, however, to make this principle explicit in his *Letters,* for his task, as he saw it, was to preserve the constituted government by threats of resistance and revolution. Junius could threaten king, Lords, and Commons with his pen, but the threats were not empty. His pen could, potentially, excite actual resistance and revolution. In the theory to which Junius subscribed, this potentiality insured that the threats would not become actualities. Thus, Junius' assertion that "the liberty of the press is the *palladium* of all the civil, political, and religious rights of an Englishmen" was not mere self-aggrandizement; it was in fact the foundation of his political beliefs.

The discrepancy between Junius' apparent republicanism and his real beliefs becomes clear in a careful reading of the following passage, which, as Junius' most explicit statement about the constitution, is worth quoting at length:

I can more readily admire the liberal spirit and integrity, than the sound judgment of any man, who prefers a republican form of government, in this or any other empire of equal extent, to a monarchy so qualified and limited as ours. I am convinced, that neither is it in theory the wisest system of government, nor practicable in this country. Yet, though I hope the English constitution will for ever preserve its original monarchical form, I would have the manners of the people purely and strictly republican. — I do not mean the licentious spirit of anarchy and riot. — I mean a general attachment to the common weal, distinct from any partial attachment to persons or families; — an implicit submission to the laws only, and an affection to the magistrate [the king], proportioned to the integrity and wisdom, with which he distributes justice to his people, and administers their affairs. The present habit of our political body appears to me the very reverse of what it ought to be. The form of the constitution leans rather more than enough to the popular branch; while, in effect, the manners of the people (of those at least who are likely to take a lead in the country) incline too generally to a dependance upon the crown. . . . It were much to be desired, that we had such men as Mr. Sawbridge to represent us in parliament. . . . He has shewn himself possessed of that republican firmness, which the times require, and by which and English gentleman may be . . . usefully and . . . honourably distinguished. . . . (p. 293).

Two elements in this passage are crucial to a proper understanding of Junius' thought. First, while it is clear that Junius rejects a republican government in favor of limited monarchy, he goes even further: the English constitution errs, if at all, in giving too much power to the "popular branch" — the House of Commons — rather than to the crown or Lords. Second, his advocacy of republican manners on the part of the people is even more limited than initially appears. He specifically condemns the kind of resistance by the populace that occurred during the Wilkes crisis — "the licentious spirit of anarchy and riot"; the populace should submit "to the laws only." Furthermore, as the passage continues, it becomes evident through the parenthetical comment and the reference to Sawbridge that Junius is advocating "republican firmness" not to the populace but to members of the House of Commons: the republican spirit is for "English gentlemen"!

A corollary of this attitude toward the populace is that men with actual political power — as opposed to the populace, which has only potential power — must be prudent about arousing the emotions of the populace over political issues. When the Supporters of the Bill of Rights passed a resolution in 1771 on the issue of American taxation, Junius reprimanded their leader, Wilkes: "I must own I think you had no business to revive a question, which should, & probably would, have lain dormant for ever" (p. 412; see also Atticus' earlier sentiment, "A wise man would have let the question drop" [Wade, II, 255]). Junius' policy on this is perfectly consistent with his political system, wherein the people are potent but largely inactive: "There are questions, which . . . you should never provoke the people in general to ask themselves" (p. 406).

IV   *Political Parties*

Junius may be justly called a Whig, though this tells us very little about him. Eighteenth-century parties were not solidly established, principled, or even respectable. Until 1770, when Burke published his *Thoughts on the Cause of the Present Discontents,* nearly everyone decried parties, or factions, as evils which ought to be eliminated. There were, of course, factions in Parliament, but the desideratum was unity; the modern notion of a loyal opposition as a positive good had not been established. Samuel Johnson praised George III as "a king who knows not the name of party, and who wishes to be the common father of all his people,"[5] and Junius, whose estimate of the king was quite different, called on him to "withdraw your confidence equally from all parties" (p. 161). Horace Walpole spoke of Pitt's "known design of uniting, that was breaking, all parties," while Pitt himself wrote to Newcastle in 1764, "I purpose to continue acting through life upon the best convictions I am able to form, and under the obligation of principles, not by the force of any particular bargains."[6] The nobility of the sentiment, if not the practicality, would have been generally admitted.

The terms "Whig" and "Tory" were commonly used, but they did not refer to a two-party system or to clearly distinguished principles. DeLolme stated in his 1784 preface that the terms had become "useless,"[7] and Johnson told Boswell that "a wise Tory and a wise Whig, I believe, will agree. Their principles are the same...."[8] Not everyone attached themselves to a party; a modern historian estimates that "barely more than a third" of the members of Parliament were connected with factions or parties.[9] Of these, the Tories were not very strong. They tended to be "country gentlemen" somewhat akin to Fielding's squires — generally opposed to government, more concerned with their dogs and local affairs than with national politics. The active politicians and leaders were all various types of Whigs who formed factions on the basis of friendship, gratitude for places or patronage, admiration for a particular leader, like Pitt, or the prospect of gaining power. It will be noted that such connections would not hold much interest for Junius himself. As an anonymous writer, known only to himself, personal ambition and gratitude were not strong motives; furthermore, Philip Francis was notoriously ungrateful to his friends and benefactors. (Junius scornfully claimed that Francis' friend Calcraft "has only determined to be a patriot, when he could not be a peer" [p. 297].) Junius did have great admiration for Grenville and Pitt, but he was much too independent to be considered one of their "party."

Parties did often form around particular issues — the party names, in fact, originated in the crisis over the Exclusion Bill in 1680–81 — but the party was seen as a temporary combination only; the party was not intended to survive the crisis. Not until Burke's *Thoughts* did anyone argue for the respectability of parties, which Burke defined as "a body of men united for promoting by their joint endeavors the national interest upon some particular principle upon which they are all agreed." By advocating party government based on respectable parties, Burke was in effect advocating a change in the actual constitution.[10]

Junius was not engaged in any such act of statesmanship; rather, he accepted the traditional view of party as an evil which was sometimes useful in particular causes. The constitutional crisis brought to a head in the Wilkes episode and its aftermath was one such cause. In trying to bring about the election of more reformers to Parliament, Junius wrote, "It is time for those, who really mean the *Cause* and the *People,* who have no view to private advantage, and who have virtue enough to prefer the general good of the community to the gratification of personal animosities, — it is time for such men to interpose" (p. 291). But this noble call to partisan action is modified later in the same letter by Junius' lack of interest in the motivating principles: "If individuals have no virtues, their vices may be of use to us. I care not with what principle the new-born patriot is animated, if the measures he supports are beneficial to the community" (p. 297). Junius was more interested in concerted action on a particular issue than in "party" in Burke's sense. But he became disillusioned in the attempt: "There are not ten men in [this country] who will unite & stand together upon any one question" (p. 393). On another occasion, he recommended that Wilkes establish "constitutional Clubs" throughout the country (p. 406) but this — like Junius' advocacy of petitions and his threats of revolution — was simply to instill the fear of the people's potential power into king, Lords, and Commons.

V   *Practical Politics*

Junius' political sense was firmly grounded on orthodox constitutional principles, but in applying these principles to political life he was above all a pragmatist. "The Lives of the best of us," he wrote, "are spent in choosing between Evils" (p. 423).

His political positions are principled, but not utopian, dogmatic, or rationalistic; they are choices among various evils. In this respect, Junius' thought is different from that of many political reformers.

An important part of his habit of mind was a lively perception of the gap between theory and practice. Some reformers were beginning to agitate on the issue of "rotten boroughs" — boroughs, like Old Sarum, which had no population but sent two members to the House of Commons. In theory, Junius agreed completely with the reformers; any defect in representation tends to corrupt and vitiate the House. But correcting the flaw involved evils as well. "It is not in human Policy to form an institution, from which no possible Inconvenience shall arise. ... We are to choose between better & worse" (p. 422). In this case, elimination of one evil must rest on the principle that Parliament has a right to disenfranchise boroughs, which Junius took to be illegal and a far greater evil. "When you propose to cut away the rotten parts, can you tell us what parts are perfectly sound? Are there any, certain, Limits, in fact or theory, to inform you at what point you must stop, — at what point the Mortification ends?" (p. 410). The possible misuse of this principle, through influence of the crown, seemed a much greater threat to Junius. Therefore, he recommended keeping the disease — the rotten boroughs — but "infusing a portion of new health into the constitution to enable it to bear its infirmities" by increasing representation where the population has increased.

Junius' mode of thought is well expressed in his letter to Wilkes on the issue of annual, triennial, or septennial parliaments: "The question is not, what is best in Theory, ... but, what is most expedient in practice. You labour to carry the Constitution to a point of perfection, which it can never reach to, or at which it cannot long be stationary. In this idea, I think I see the Mistake of a speculative Man ..." (p. 421).

One of Junius' most unpopular stands was his support of the crown's right to impress seamen into naval service. The London city politicians were offering bounties to attract volunteers in order to fill their quota and were protesting the right of impressment. Junius was doubly embarrassed by his support of impressment: not only was it a clear invasion of an individual's liberty, it was also supported by his archenemy Lord Mansfield. But again, Junius saw the issue as a choice between two evils — lessening the individual's liberty, on the one hand, as opposed to hazarding the safety of the nation, on the other. He chose the former as the lesser evil and again resorted to his disease metaphor: the symptoms "may ... be softened" by offering bounties to the extent that the public purse will allow, but "the distemper cannot be cured"; the king must have the right to impress in order to maintain the security of the state. "The community has a right to command, as well as to purchase, the service of its members. ... There is no remedy, in the nature of things, for the grievance complained of; for, if there were, it must long since have been redressed. ... Let bounties be increased as far as the public purse can support them. Still they have a limit; and when every reasonable expence is incurred, it will be found, in fact, that the spur of the press is wanted to give operation to the bounty" (p. 295). On this point Junius had to part company with Wilkes and the London politicians. Having wrestled with the issue and determined his position, he refused to yield.

In these examples we see Junius' mind at work in an impressive and typical way. He starts with a solid grasp of the principles from which he reasons, moves on to a clear comprehension of the facts and implications of the immediate political issue, and finally arrives at a firm, hardheaded, clearly reasoned statement of his stand on the issue, a stand which is at once principled and pragmatic. This is not Junius' only mode of thought — his satiric portraits of Grafton reveal quite another — but it is certainly his most humane and most admirable.

CHAPTER 7

The Art of Persuasion

I T has been seen that Junius as a polemicist had many advantages which help account for his success: a carefully protected anonymity; a strong conviction in a single thesis about the decline of the nation; the existence of various important issues, both domestic and foreign, by which to capture the attention of the populace; and a firm set of political principles from which to argue and attack. These advantages were crucial to the notoriety and power that Junius attained; without any one of them his effectiveness would have been considerably weakened. But even in their cumulative force, these advantages cannot explain the phenomenon of Junius. Indeed, they would count for very little without Junius' rhetorical genius.

In an age when political letter writers were abundant, Junius clearly stood out from the horde because of his literary art. Johnson's comment, "I know no man but Burke who is capable of writing these letters,"[1] was no mean tribute, since Burke was recognized as the greatest political writer of his age. Literary historians have seconded Johnson's grudging admiration of the *Letters*. C. W. Previté-Orton, in the *Cambridge History of English Literature*, mentions Junius' "evil taint," his "personal hatred," his "rancour," but concludes that "Junius holds a high position on his own literary merits. He was the most perfect wielder of slanderous polemic that had ever arisen in English political controversy. Not lack of rivals, but eminent ability, made him supreme in that ignoble competition."[2] Similarly, but less grudgingly, D. Nichol Smith said that the *Letters* "in their invective and general mastery of rhetorical device were the most effective political contributions to any newspaper of the century."[3]

The *Letters* do in fact display a "general mastery of rhetorical device," but there are two reasons why readers acknowledge the

110

mastery only grudgingly or not at all. First, some readers deplore envenomed attack, no matter how skillfully executed, and second, some readers prefer a more expansive, philosophical style to Junius' pointed, concrete style. Although Burke was suspected of writing the *Letters,* his style is usually so different from Junius' that many who admire Burke cannot abide Junius — and vice versa. "One reader does not like the neatness of Junius," Hazlitt observed, "and another objects to the extravagance of Burke."[4] Some critics combine both objections in their judgment of the *Letters.* "The literary value of Junius seems to have been absurdly overrated," according to Edmund Gosse. There is too much "malignity," no "philosophical enthusiasm"; he is "personal first and patriotic afterwards."[5] The most dazzling anti-Junius critic is Thomas DeQuincey, who eloquently elevates Burke and denigrates Junius, allowing him only

one talent, undoutedly, . . . in a rare perfection — the talent of sarcasm. He stung like a scorpion. . . . Rhetorician he was none; for, without sentiment, without imagery, without generalization, how should it be possible for rhetoric to subsist? . . . Junius has not one principle, aphorism, or remark of a general nature in his whole armoury; not in a single solitary instance sis his barren understanding ascend to an abstraction or general idea, but lingered for ever in the dust and rubbish of individuality, amongst the tangible realities of things and persons.[6]

Such objections perhaps admit to no answer; to point out that "malignity" is not uncommon in satire is a weak rejoinder to this vehemence. If one thinks of rhetoric, however, with Aristotle, not as sentiments, imagery, or generalizations, but as the choices the author makes in establishing his ethos as speaker, in characterizing his audience, and in presenting his argument, Junius' distinctive mastery may be appreciated for what it is. Malice abounds in the letters, and no doubt did in the author, but it is transformed by Junius' skill into a controlled, calculated malignity that moved readers to excitement, fear, and anger.

I *Junius' Self-Portrait*

Writing excellent letters that catch the attention of the public and move them to action is a rare talent; possessing it, Junius could afford to be scornful of the run-of-the-mill writers of political letters — a "Set of Brutes" whose style is "too dull" and whose measures are "too gross" to merit any attention (p. 351). His own letters, as he made abundantly clear in his private correspondence with Woodfall, were usually written with careful deliberation: "The inclosed ... has been greatly laboured" (p. 364); another is "finished with the utmost Care" (p. 372); still another is written "I assure you with no small labour" (p. 374). His grand pronouncement, "I weigh every word ..." (p. 382), was no doubt intended to discourage his publisher from making any alterations, but his statement to Wilkes has the ring of sincerity: "The pains I took with that paper upon privilege [Letter XLIV] were greater than I can express to you" (p. 421).

To his publisher and to his reading public Junius presented himself as personally and politically independent. He refused any payment or royalties from Woodfall, promised to take care of his expenses in case of a lawsuit, and took pains to dissociate himself from factions — notably Wilkes' or Chatham's. Although Francis made only a small salary and had no easy time meeting his expenses, Junius appeared to be independently wealthy: "My Rank and Fortune," he proclaimed, "place me above a common Bribe" (p. 457).

This lordly demeanor, however, although useful occasionally, was not often exploited; indeed, the reference to exalted "Rank and Fortune" was omitted from the collected *Letters*. Much more prominent is his claim to be enlisted in the cause of "the people." "I speak to the people as one of the people" (p. 292). He often contrasts himself as a certain kind of speaker vis-à-vis his antagonists. Sir William Draper, as characterized by Junius, is a "scholar," whose "academical education has given [him] an unlimited command over the most beautiful figures of speech" — Junius is being ironic here — and who writes Latin "with almost as much purity as English." Junius, on the contrary, is but "a plain unlettered man" (p. 51). Likewise, the ministerial apologists who publish pamphlets are compared unfavorably to the letter-writing Junius. "They pile up reluctant quarto upon solid folio, as if their labours, because they are gigantic, could contend with truth and heaven." In contrast, Junius presents himself as virtuously humble: "Mine, I confess, are humble labours. I do not presume to instruct the learned, but simply to inform the body of people; and I prefer that channel of conveyance [that is, newspapers], which is likely to spread farthest among them" (p. 106).

Lacking the academic flowers of a Draper or the lengthy

pomposity of a ministerial writer, Junius' writing instead displays fervent passions which respond to "the *Cause* and the *People.*" He advertises his scorn for moderation (that "shameful indifference about the interests of society" [p. 230]), and thus makes his malignity a virtue: "Forgive this passionate language. — I am unable to correct it. — The subject comes home to us all. — It is the language of my heart" (p. 290).

Junius' most salient trait, however, is his singular lack of identity — his anonymity. This was, of course, primarily a way of protecting himself: Philip Francis could not have been discovered without losing his position in government and perhaps much else besides. But, as he well knew, his secrecy was also an invaluable rhetorical device. Signed "Philip Francis," the letters would have been widely read, but the inevitable curiosity about the remarkable author would have been easily satisfied. Signed "Junius," they raised insatiable curiosity, inspired many answers, and confirmed none. The mystery spread, stimulating more interest in the anonymous productions, and evoking an awesome respect for the mystery, if not the politics, of the author. The anonymity, in short, became a crucial part of Junius' rhetorical character: "Stat nominis umbra" ("He stands the shadow of a name"). Junius was, of course, delighted with the effectiveness of this role. "At present there is something oracular in the delivery of my opinions," he wrote to Wilkes. "I speak from a Recess, which no human Curiosity can penetrate; & Darkness, we are told,' is one Source of the Sublime. — The Mystery of *Junius* increases his Importance" (p. 424).

Junius' anonymity, however, was a dangerous rhetorical device precisely because it allowed the unknown author to be shameless: he could be greedy, partial, ambitious, even vicious, without having to suffer the consequences. If his antagonists could equate Junius and cowardice, the dignity of his mystery would be dispelled. Sir William Draper and Horne Tooke tried, but failed; Junius was careful to guard his character from this challenge. "To write for profit without taxing the press; — to write for fame and to be unknown; — to support the intrigues of faction and to be disowned, as a dangerous auxiliary, by every party in the kingdom, are contradictions, which the minister must reconcile, before I forfeit my credit with the public" (p. 228). When Horne Tooke accused him of remaining aloof from the action, avoiding the danger of political battle, Junius responded, "Whenever *Junius* ap-

pears, he must encounter a host of enemies. . . . Is there no merit in
dedicating my life to the information of my fellow-subjects? —
What public question have I declined, what villain have I spared?''
Indeed, the exchange between Junius and Horne Tooke became a
celebrated rhetorical duel, more interesting for the parrying of well-
matched antagonists than for their arguments. "Is there no labour
in the composition of these letters!" Junius asked. "Mr. Horne, I
fear, . . . measures the facility of *my* writings, by the fluency of his
own" (p. 273). Horne Tooke's rejoinder is the classic anti-Sophist
argument: "I compassionate your labour in the composition of
your letters, and will communicate to you the secret of my fluency.
— Truth needs no ornament; and, in my opinion, what she borrows
of the pencil is deformity" (p. 281). Rhetoric is deformity, according to this reasoning; it obscures rather than reveals truth.

Junius clearly rejected this scorn for rhetoric. In his view, the
task facing him was not merely to state the truth about the ministry
and the state of England, though that was certainly part of it. He
also, however, had to persuade the audience of this truth and move
them to action. This requires the skill of "the pencil," and Junius
was highly sensitive to such skill. For example, when Junius
criticized Wilkes' group for its long political resolution, he objected
not only to substantive matters but also gave them an incisive lesson on their rhetorical handling of the ethos of the speaker: "You
talk of yourselves with too much Authority & Importance. By
assuming this false Pomp and Air of Consequence, you either give
general Disgust, or, what is infinitely more dangerous, you expose
yourselves to be laughed at. The English are a fastidious people, &
will not submit to be talked to, in so high a Tone, by a Set of
private Gentlemen, of whom they know nothing, but that they call
themselves *Supporters of the Bill of Rights*" (p. 406). On another
instance Junius rewrote a message Wilkes intended to send to the
lord mayor. The meaning was nearly the same but, in Junius' view,
the rewritten version was "not less strong than your own Words, &
better guarded in point of safety, which you neglect too much"
(p. 431). The *manner* as well as the *matter,* in Junius' view, is crucial to the art of writing.

II   *Speaker and Audience*

Junius' "Dedication to the English Nation," which prefaces the
collected *Letters,* is primarily a rhetorical act intended to establish

the relation between himself and his audience. The possibilities for this relation are numerous; the political writer can attempt to be humbly subservient to his audience, browbeat them, flatter them, speak with superior cynicism or learned authority, plead passionately, alarm with jeremiads, and so forth. Junius' choice is masterful; it is founded on the relationship established throughout the three previous years when the letters had appeared in the *Public Advertiser,* yet convincingly develops the complex relation in a single essay.

The essay begins with one of Junius' characteristic postures as one of the people ("I dedicate to You a collection of Letters, written by one of Yourselves for the common benefit of us all") and proceeds in a humble, self-deprecating strain: "To me they originally owe nothing, but a healthy, sanguine constitution. Under *Your* care they have thriven. To *You* they are indebted for whatever strength or beauty they possess" (p. 7). Junius is engaged in a delicate balancing act, complimenting his audience on the one hand, and praising the strength, beauty, and "principles worthy to be transmitted to posterity" of his own productions, on the other. But the trump card is his aggressive humility which concludes the first paragraph: "This is not the language of vanity. If I am a vain man, my gratification lies within a narrow circle. I am the sole depositary of my own secret, and it shall perish with me." He is, in short, an extraordinary, awesome mystery.

From this foundation Junius goes on to characterize himself as an honest, hard-working, passionate man ("Let me exhort and conjure You never to suffer an invasion of Your political constitution") and continues with forthright, man-to-man talk with his readers ("It may be nearer perhaps than any of us expect, and I would warn You to be prepared for it"). He gradually becomes more didactic, assuming the role of the lofty, formal teacher ("Let it be impressed upon your minds, let it be instilled into your children, that the liberty of the press is the *Palladium* of all the civil, political, and religious rights of an Englishman"), but sprinkling his instruction with expressions of confidence in his readers ("I cannot doubt that You will unanimously assert the freedom of election. . . . I am persuaded You will not leave it to the choice of seven hundred persons, notoriously corrupted by the crown . . .").

After describing the evil of "long parliaments [which] are the foundation of the undue influence of the crown," he concludes his essay with an impassioned call to action: "But the inattention or indifference of the nation has continued too long. You are roused at last to a sense of your danger. — The remedy will soon be in your power. If *Junius* lives, You shall often be reminded of it. If, when the opportunity presents itself, You neglect to do your duty to yourselves and to posterity, — to God and to your country, I shall have one consolation left, in common with the meanest and basest of mankind. — Civil liberty may still last the life of JUNIUS." By this point, Junius has transformed the rhetorical situation entirely: far from the deferential, modest writer or the patient instructor, he is now the prophet of freedom who may or may not be heard. He has done *his* part — he has roused the people from their apathy; it is now their part to act. Mindful of past, present, and future, of the individual, God, and country, Junius conjures up an image of himself in the event that the audience should fail to respond to his challenge: linked to the lowest of the people, he will also be their antithesis, a prophet become martyr, dying unheard in the noble struggle, deserted by an audience which has forfeited its freedom.

These qualities of the speaker and attitudes toward the audience recur throughout the letters, skillfully manipulated by the author to create a strong effect. They are appeals to popular opinion, passionate and active rather than intellectual or meditative. As Coleridge rightly observed, the letters "impel to action, not thought."[8]

One of Junius' most perceptive contemporary commentators was a letter writer who called himself "Alciphron." "The admiration that is so lavishly bestowed upon [Junius]," he wrote, "affords one of the clearest proofs, perhaps, that can be found, how much more easily men are swayed by imagination, than by judgment; and that a fertile invention, glittering language, and sounding periods, act with far greater force upon the mind, than the simple deductions of sober reasoning, or the calm evidence of facts. ... His readers are persuaded because they are agitated, and convinced because they are pleased."[9] Junius' persuasive imagination and "fertile invention" found its natural expression in the form of satire.

III   *The Letters as Satire*

If the rhetoric of the "Dedication" does not strike us as Junius at his best, it is because it lacks the irony and wit that inform the controlled malice of Junius' best work. "I am not conversant in the language of panegyric," he confessed (p. 275). Junius was a good hater, but, more important, he was capable of transforming his hatred into literary form. Coleridge suggested a useful approach to Junius: "Perhaps the fair way of considering these Letters would be as a kind of satirical poems; the short, and for ever balanced, sentences constitute a true metre; and the connection is that of satiric poetry, a witty logic, as association of thoughts by amusing semblances of cause and effect, the sophistry of which the reader has an interest in not stopping to detect, for it flatters his love of mischief, and makes the sport."[10] His métier lay in various forms of satire — invective, the "character," the ironic arguments, mock praise, diminishing wit, and dramatic farce.[11]

It has already been pointed out in chapter 1 that despite the topical, immediate politics of the letters, Junius to some extent creates "imagined worlds" by which to forward his attacks; that is, he suspends the world of political fact to enter the world of literary fiction. At these moments, his concern is still with his immediate political objectives; his technique of achieving them simply changes. Junius' entry into the world of satire is always at the expense of a living victim like Grafton, Mansfield, or the king. He does not fear using the lash; the cry of *"Measures and not men"* is, he says, "the common cant of affected moderation; — a base, counterfeit language, fabricated by knaves, and made current among fools" (p. 130 n.).

Junius' choice of words clearly places him in the tradition of Swift's and Pope's satiric worlds, peopled by knaves and fools. In such a world the satirist is one of the endangered, perhaps nearly extinct, species who has common sense, can perceive simple distinctions of right and wrong, and can be outraged at the triumph of evil. In the satiric world, moral truth is turned topsy-turvy, madmen become the norm, and knaves become prime ministers. Where Pope perceives Chaos and Universal Darkness, Junius perceives the spread of "the present degenerate state of society." At such a time the satirist becomes himself a fool if he allows individual knaves to escape with impunity, gain more power, and retain the favor of the crown. It is revealing that Junius defends his attack on individuals by quoting Pope: " 'To reform and not to chastise I am afraid, is impossible.... To attack vices in the abstract, without touching persons, may be safe fighting indeed, but it is fighting with shadows. My greatest comfort and encouragement to proceed has been to see that those, who have no shame, and no fear of any thing else, have appeared touched by my satires' " (p. 130 n.). Such "comfort" may be termed the true pride of the satirist. Junius, in confident moments, feels more than a touch of it: even "his Majesty ... has honoured the *Public Advertiser* with particular attention," and, he ironically continues, "the gracious character of the best of Princes is by this time not only perfectly known to his subjects, but tolerably well understood by the rest of Europe" (p. 251) — largely, we infer, because of Junius.

One primitive form of satire is invective, a form not uncommon in eighteenth-century politics. We have seen in chapter 4 the particular invectives hurled against Grafton and Mansfield. It is clear that Junius took considerable relish in verbal abuse; Draper called him the "high priest of envy, malice, and all uncharitableness." Warming up to an attack on Mansfield, Junius writes, "Our language has no term of reproach, the mind has no idea of detestation, which has not already been happily applied to you, and exhausted. — Ample justice has been done by abler pens than mine to the separate merits of your life and character. Let it be *my* humble office to collect the scattered sweets, till their united virtue tortures the sense" (p. 207). Indeed, Junius' invective hits the mark when it is characterized by this relish and verbal dexterity. Otherwise, as in his attacks on Barrington, it is merely gross and malicious. More often than not, Junius' antagonists (Draper, for example), rather than Junius, are driven to simple invective as their means of attack. Junius' more temperate alter ego, Philo-Junius, wrote to Zeno, a defender of Mansfield, "I will not call you *liar, jesuit,* or *villain* [as Zeno had called Junius]; but, with all the politeness imaginable, perhaps I may prove you so" (p. 302).

At his best, Junius makes his invective an integral part of a satiric "character," a literary portrait revealing the essential traits of a person. The tradition was a rich one in the satire preceding Junius: Samuel Butler's *Characters* in prose, and in poetry Dryden's Zimri, Pope's Atticus and Sporus, and Swift's Wharton, to mention only a few. Junius' characters bear just enough resemblance to the real person to establish a degree of validity, but their richness lies in Junius' witty fabrications. The results prompted a perceptive appreciation by Coleridge: "One of Junius' arts, and which gives me a high notion of his genius, as a poet and satirist, is this: he takes for granted the existence of a character that never did and never can exist, and then employs his wit, and surprises and amuses his readers with analyzing and setting forth its incompatibilities."[12] Draper, who early entered the fray against Junius without quite realizing his special genius, complained bitterly that "this uncandid indecent writer has gone so far as to turn one of the most amiable men of the age [Granby] into a stupid, unfeeling, and senseless being; possessed indeed of a personal courage, but void of those essential qualities which distinguish the commander from the common soldier" (p. 35). Draper, looking for literal truth, found the portraits "indecent"; Coleridge, looking for satire, found them superb. Draper, of course, became himself the victim of Junius' powerful satiric fictions.

Throughout the letters Junius was especially concerned with creating a character of Grafton, the fineness of which prompted Coleridge's appreciation. At the outset Junius approaches his subject with a clinical zest — "Let me be permitted to consider your character and conduct merely as a subject of curious speculation" (p. 68). He builds his fiction around Grafton's alleged consistent inconsistency: his inevitable betrayal of friends and changes of policy. The portrait evolves as Junius moves from issue to issue: "In your treatment of particular persons, you have preserved the uniformity of your character. Even Mr. Bradshaw [for whom Grafton obtained a large pension] declares, that no man was ever so ill used as himself" (p. 178). Even when Grafton *fails* to do evil, Junius finds material for witty damnation. When he dropped what Junius considered an unjust prosecution, Grafton was charged with abdicating his "brave determination" to be stupidly evil: "You have now added the last negative to your character" (p. 180). Even Grafton's sympathy for a friend's failure in litigation, which Grafton prompted, is attacked with perverse irony. "My Lord; — I am a little anxious for the consistency of your character. You violate your own rules of decorum, when you do not insult the man, whom you have betrayed" (p. 316). Such convoluted twists of nonfacts have nothing to do with reality; they are sports of Junius' imagination. Nonetheless, as Alciphron commented, readers are "convinced because they are pleased." For the relish of this witty malice, the reader willingly suspends his disbelief, and Junius' "characters" take on a life of their own.

A stock device of the Augustan satirists and of Junius is mock praise. Of the dunce poet Dryden writes: "Shadwell alone of all my sons is he / Who stands confirmed in full stupidity. / The rest to some faint meaning make pretense, / But Shadwell never deviates into sense."[13] Echoing Dryden, Junius praises Grafton for his perfection: "The most accomplished persons have usually some defect, some weakness in their characters.... Tiberius had his forms; Charteris now and then deviated into honesty; and even Lord B[altimor]e prefers the simplicity of seduction to the poignant pleasures of a rape. But yours, my Lord, is a perfect character: through every line of public and private life you are consistent with yourself" (p. 517; Wade, II, 172). The same mock praise plays around his often repeated reference to "our gracious Sovereign" and his characterization of Hillsborough as "the darling child of prudence and urbanity" (Wade, II, 233).

Occasionally, though under a different name, Junius varies his witty attack by using farce, in the tradition of Pope, Arbuthnot, and Fielding. When Barrington appointed Anthony Chamier ("Tony Shammy") to be deputy secretary at war, Junius, alias Veteran, dramatized Barrington sending a lieutenant general to his subordinates: *"My dear General, I'm prodigiously hurried. But do me the Favour to go to Mr. Shammy; ... go to my Duckling; go to little Three per cents reduced; you'll find him ... an* OMNIUM *of all that's genteel; the Activity of a Broker; the Politeness of a Hair-dresser ..."* (p. 497). Several of the Veteran letters are actually playlets, with stage directions and farcical dialogue, combined into preposterous episodes at the expense of Barrington.

IV   *Junius on Argumentation*

Junius' basic appeal, according to Alciphron, is not to the judgment but to the imagination: he "affirms without reason, and decides without proof." Despite his high praise of the common sense of the "people," Junius' assumption that the people need not be expected to *think* is not flattering. Yet Alciphron was essentially correct about the main force of the letters. It is not accidental that the letter form which Junius chose does not lend itself to extended argument and proofs but does lend itself to displays of wit, incisive attacks, and calls to action.

Junius did have some intellectual justification for minimizing the appeal to reason. In the first place, as observed in chapter 6, Junius believed that the people could *feel* political evils and exert, or threaten, enough force that the evils would be ameliorated. They need not reason about political causes and effects; indeed, they probably did not have the training, experience, or information to do so. Therefore, Junius' attempts to influence the populace — and through them the House of Commons or ministry — were largely by nonrational appeals.

In the second place, Junius was profoundly suspicious of elaborate argumentation; it appeared to him to be often a means of deception rather than a means of getting at the truth. When he speaks of an argument "full of subtlety and refinement," he is damning rather than praising it (pp. 98, 99). He contrasts the simple "evidence of the senses" with the "persuasion of argument" and, finding them often at odds, prefers the former. The attempt of the ministry to expel Wilkes by various legal arguments particularly incensed Junius. He published one letter contrasting three "facts," both simple and true, according to Junius, with three ministerial "arguments," sophisticated deceptions. He called his letter, parodying eighteenth-century pamphlet titles, "ARGUMENT against FACT; or, A new system of political Logic, by which the ministry have demonstrated, to the satisfaction of their friends, that expulsion alone creates a complete incapacity to be reelected" (p. 112).

Like Swift, Junius combines a scorn for elaborate reasoning with a detestation of lawyers. Referring to the Wilkes question in particular — but also to all attempts to get at truth — he wrote, "In this, as in almost every other dispute, it usually happens that much time is lost in referring to a multitude of cases and precedents, which prove nothing to the purpose, or in maintaining propositions, which are either not disputed, or . . . are entirely indifferent as to the matter in debate; until at last the mind, perplexed and confounded with the endless subtleties of controversy, loses sight of the main question, and never arrives at truth" (pp. 86–87). Junius, as the plain-speaking man of common sense, one of the people, seldom threatens to lead his readers into the "endless subtleties of controversy." The lawyer, on the other hand, is a snake, practiced in deception. With cutting irony, Junius addresses Blackstone: "You are a lawyer, Sir, and know better than I do, upon what particular occasions a talent for misrepresentation may be *fairly* exerted" (p. 95); to Junius and people of common sense, misrepresentation in argument is never "fair." "The indiscriminate defence of right and wrong," he instructs Mansfield, "contracts the understanding, while it corrupts the heart" (p. 323).

When Junius does engage in argumentation, the results can be brilliant. His natural and most effective mode is the argument from cause and effect. Letter I, for example, the sweeping damnation of the ministry, begins with an argument from effect to cause: trade has decayed, dissensions have sprung up throughout the empire, England has lost the respect of foreign powers, and the people are desperate. In such a case we need "look no farther for the true cause of every mischief that befals us": it is a "weak, distracted, and corrupt" government (pp. 26–27). The letter then continues with various arguments from cause to effect: an inexperienced, gambling young nobleman has been made minister of finance and sunk the nation into debt; a series of ill-considered, inconsistent laws has alienated the American colonies from England; and so forth — examples designed to link the ministers (the causes) with the state of the nation (the effect).

This causal mode of argument seems to be the natural bent of Junius' mind. He is interested in tracing particular political acts or the state of the nation back to their origins, and he usually assumes that the cause of any given act will be found in a single person, rather than in a complex combination of social forces. Or, he is interested in analyzing a particular political act, such as the expulsion of Wilkes from Commons or a libel suit against the publisher Woodfall, and project the political consequences of the act. This mode of argument is most conducive to the satiric "character." Junius can argue from the effects of Grafton's ministry back to Grafton's corrupt character, or from his corrupt character to the disastrous effects of his power in England. This cast of mind — perfect though it is for this kind of political satire — is not philosophic or elevated. "It was the degrading necessity of Sir Philip Francis' mind," said DeQuincey, "to lower the universal to the particular."[14] Junius' arguments, though often about fundamental issues, seldom leave the realm of the particular, the here-and-now.

Junius sometimes employed the mode of argument from circumstances, and it is at these times — when discussing rotten boroughs, the impressment of sailors, or the American colonies — that he sounds most like Burke. Despite his formidable satiric malice, Junius is much more tolerant of evil than was a political radical like Thomas Paine. The radical of the late eighteenth century was concerned with the "rights of man," which the impressment of sailors clearly violated; therefore, to him impressment would be a form of tyranny and should be abolished. Junius recognizes the force of this argument, but is finally carried by the argument from circumstance: rights or no rights, sailors are essential; what must be, must be. Junius occasionally employs the argument from genus, typical of Paine, arguing that something does or does not belong to the class of what is "constitutional" or a "right." There is a simplicity and immediacy about this mode of argument that makes it an attractive possibility for the letter writer; thus, it is used more often in the letters than the argument from circumstance, but it is not finally as important a part of Junius' manner of thinking.

In keeping with his ethos as the independent man of common sense, Junius seldom uses the argument from authority, the argument that his position is the best because it is supported by the Bible, a philosopher, a great politician, or a statute. His attempt to convict Mansfield of an illegal act led him to write a long argument (Letter LXVIII) almost exclusively based on legal authorities, but it is an intolerably dull letter (as Junius himself confessed), and wrong as well, ironically confirming Junius' distrust of such arguments.

V The "Address to the King"

Junius' rhetorical triumph was Letter XXXV, the "Address to the King," published on December 19, 1769. The letter created a sensation throughout England; the *Public Advertiser* sold more copies than ever before in its history, and all the nonministerial papers, as well as the radical magazines, reprinted it. Almost immediately, the government pronounced it libelous. Burke's reaction, spoken in the House of Commons, suggests the powerful effect the letter had on its contemporary audience: "For my part, when I saw [Junius'] attack upon the king, I own my blood ran cold. I thought he had ventured too far, and there was an end of his triumphs, not that he had not asserted many truths. Yes, Sir, there are in that composition many bold truths, by which a wise prince might profit."[15]

The letter as a whole is labeled "For the *Public Advertiser,*" but nine-tenths of it is a letter addressed to the king. The introductory paragraph evokes a state of urgency in which the "security of the Sovereign" and the "general safety of the state" are endangered, then establishes the fictional circumstance, confessedly "improbable," wherein an "honest man" could address a king who, because of his danger, suddenly recognizes his disgrace and his duty to his subjects. This king has "spirit enough" to bid his subject speak freely and "understanding enough" to listen with attention. The overelaborate fiction — "it may be a matter of curious SPECULATION" — combined with the obvious relevance of this speculation to England and George III, holds an insult to the king without directly stating it.

The actual address to the king falls into six sections, the first three dealing with the past — the people's former attitude toward the king, the king's mistakes attributable to others (his tutors and ministers), and the king's own mistakes in the Wilkes affair — and the second three dealing with the future — the king's potential allies in a revolution, the alternatives open to him in the Wilkes case, and a conclusion of warning to the king. The letter in the first part becomes increasingly critical of the king, building toward the audacious central section in which Junius considers who will be opposed to the king in a revolution — Ireland, the American colonies, the English people, and the army — and who will support him — "all the Jacobites, Non-jurors, Roman Catholics, and Tories of this country, and all Scotland without exception" (p. 167). Thus his advice to the king to renounce his ministers and Parliament, dissolve Parliament, acknowledge his own mistakes, and free Wilkes from prison with a complete pardon is flanked by threats of revolution. The letter ends by referring to George's Stuart predecessors, one of whom had lost his head by revolution and another his throne: "The Prince, who imitates their conduct, should be warned by their example; and while he plumes himself upon the security of his title to the crown, should remember that, as it was acquired by one revolution, it may be lost by another" (p. 173).

The chances that the king might undergo a sudden transformation of character or adopt Junius' advice, were nil; the basic assumption of the letter is more than "improbable." Furthermore, Junius' rhetorical arrangement, not to mention the substance of his arguments, did nothing to increase those chances. Although the ostensible audience of this letter is the king, the real audience is quite different. To a large extent he is addressing the English people, instructing them again about the state of the nation and especially the Wilkes case. While he is not trying to urge the people to revolution, he does want to fan their spirit of resistance and make them aware of their *potential* power. But he is also addressing the Parliament, ministry, and king, not to persuade them by his logic, but to make them feel the threat of the people's potential power as a check on the government's actual power.

The people and their potential power are displayed in the opening sentence: "When the complaints of a brave and powerful people are observed to encrease in proportion to the wrongs they have suffered; when, instead of sinking into submission, they are roused to resistance, the time will soon arrive at which every inferior consideration must yield to the security of the Sovereign, and to the general safety of the state.'' They are characterized as an oppressed people, about to assert their rights manfully in just rebellion. Yet when Junius addresses the king, the people for whom he speaks appear to be reasonable, generous, and affectionate: "We are still inclined to make an indulgent allowance for the pernicious lessons you received in your youth . . .''; "We separate the amicable, good-natured prince from the folly and treachery of his servants . . .''; of the Peace of Paris, "On *your* part we are satisfied that every thing was honourable and sincere, and if England was sold to France, we doubt not that your Majesty was equally betrayed''; "Far from suspecting you of so horrible a design [as settling the Wilkes' case by force], we would attribute the continued violation of the laws, and even this last enormous attack upon the vital principles of the constitution, to an ill-advised, unworthy personal resentment'' (pp. 160–64). As the professions are repeated, however, the reader (including the people — "we" — themselves) gets the impression that the people are unreasonably reasonable, kind to a fault, overly generous, and finally that they know more about the king's corruption than they pretend to know: the irony insinuates itself subtly but effectively. And, contrary to these professions of trust in the king, Junius speaks of revolution as if it were imminent.

The paragraph in which he considers the Scots as the king's potential supporters in a revolution reveals many of the virtues of the letter as a whole. This and the last two paragraphs are also of special interest in that they are singled out by Coleridge as "perhaps the finest paragraphs in the whole collection [of Junius' letters]."[16] Junius opens by referring again to the king's early education, this time in a less tolerant light:

As to the Scotch, I must suppose your heart and understanding so biassed, from your earliest infancy, in their favour, that nothing less than *your own* misfortunes can undeceive you. You will not accept of the uniform experience of your ancestors; and when once a man is determined to believe, the very absurdity of the doctrine confirms him in his faith. A bigoted understanding can draw a proof of attachment to the house of Hanover from a notorious zeal for the house of Stuart, and find an earnest of future loyalty in former rebellions. (p. 168)

After the directness of the initial sentence, which suggests a certain denseness in the king, Junius moves to a metaphorical plane. Using religious imagery, he deftly transforms the king from a faithful believer in absurd doctrine into the bigot: only this can explain the zany illogic of a Hanover devoted to rebels in the Stuart cause. Political attacks may degenerate into ranting invective, but Junius' attacks, at their best, evolve into witty and detached sport. In this passage, he is clearly playing with words, and the delight of them — not their truth — carries conviction to the reader.

Yet there is some truth in the incongruity of a Hanover attached to former Stuart rebels, and Junius wittily pursues it: "One would think they had forgotten that you are their lawful King, and had mistaken you for a pretender to the crown." The incongruity is "solved," however, by Junius' analysis of the Scots' sincere fickleness, exemplified by their treatment of Charles I, the Stuart who lost his head. From this pertinent historical digression, Junius returns to the case at hand:

A wise prince might draw from it two lessons of equal utility to himself. On one side he might learn to dread the undisguised resentment of a generous people, who dare openly assert their rights, and who, in a just cause are ready to meet their Sovereign in the field. On the other side, he would be taught to apprehend something far more formidable; — a fawning treachery, against which no prudence can guard, no courage can defend. The insidious smile upon the cheek would warn him of the canker in the heart.

The paragraph, at its close, has moved back to the seriousness with which it began; Junius uses English Charles, as Johnson had used Swedish Charles, to "point a moral or adorn a tale." The "lessons" are kept in the hypothetical future, yet firmly grounded in history; the English people are both "generous" and threatening; the Scotch are far more threatening and far less noble; and the whole culminates in a short, pithy sentence whose balanced parts and metaphor form an epigrammatic sneer.

The pithy sentence is in fact the hallmark of Junius' style. As Coleridge more than once observed, Junius could not handle a long sentence. But of the short, hard-hitting, unqualified sentence, Junius was a master. Although Junius' thought is never profound or original, but commonplace enough to be easily accessible to a wide readership, the style calls attention to itself by its singularity; it demands to be read. Through his choice of diction Junius characteristically achieves a cutting scorn in his adjectives, as in "a fawning treachery" and "the insidious smile" in the passage quoted above. Within the short sentence Junius also employs considerable balance, parallelism, and antithesis, emphasizing his meaning without detracting from the immediacy of it.

These traits, along with his metaphors and his series of rhetorical questions, create a prose which is memorable and damning even when it has little basis in literal truth. And, most noticeably, it is full of Junius' characteristic malignity. However much "evil taint" or "rancor" one wishes to charge to Philip Francis, Junius was successful because his malignity was carefully created, then controlled, by the art of the rhetorician.

CHAPTER 8

Francis After Junius

P HILIP FRANCIS published his last Junius letter in January,
1772, resigned from the War Office, attacked his employer,
Lord Barrington, in the Veteran letters, then set out for his travels
on the Continent. On his return he wrote one last, embittered letter
to his publisher Woodfall, informing him that Junius would write
no more. In 1773, through the help of the unsuspecting Barrington,
who wrote a flattering recommendation to Lord North, Francis
was appointed to a position on the powerful Bengal Council at a
salary of 1000 pounds a year. The king had heard favorable reports
of Francis' work in the War Office and was pleased to make the appointment; he had no inkling that he was rewarding his most
shameless enemy. Thus began a new phase in the life of Francis.
His principles and passions, which continued every bit as strong as
they had been, operated now not primarily in the realm of anonymous newspaper columns but in the world of public officialdom,
first as Bengal councillor, then as member of Parliament.

I *Francis and India*

By 1773 the East India Company had become the most
formidable power in India and, next to the Bank of England, the
richest institution in England. Due both to an influence that had
spread over a considerable portion of India and to a steadily increasing trade, the "nabobs" of the company were returning to England with enormous fortunes. Yet the company's problems were
formidable as a consequence of its having been drawn into the task
of governing as well as trading. It carried on wars, taxed,
administered justice — all in the interest of profits. But, despite its
power, it was on the verge of bankruptcy. Parliament finally
stepped in to bring the private company under some government
control. The result was North's Regulating Act, which aided the

company with loans and favorable customs benefits, set up a new judicial system, with Elijah Impey as chief justice, and reconstituted the governing power. The Bengal presidency, consisting of a governor-general and a council, was made supreme over Madras and Bombay.

Warren Hastings was already the governor-general, but by North's Act his power was transferred to the council, of which he was one member of five. As it happened, three of the newly appointed members — Francis, Clavering, and Monson — formed a majority in opposition to Hastings. When they reached India, after the six-month boat trip, they immediately set about overturning Hastings' policies. Francis was clearly the intellectual leader of the majority, and he soon proved to be Hastings' personal antagonist. During the years Francis was in India (1774–80), and for years afterward, the two were in conflict. Although both were men of brilliance and integrity — neither, unlike many "nabobs," was a mere fortune hunter — their tactics and principles were entirely different.

As a councillor, Francis was forced to write a great deal in order to maintain contacts with England. His writing, like Junius', was of very high quality. Of Francis' *Plan of Settlement* (1782), originally written as minutes of the Bengal Council, Burke said, "I don't know that I ever read any State paper drawn with more ability; and indeed I have seldom read a paper of any kind with more pleasure."[1] One of Francis' longest pamphlets was a communiqué of 1777, later republished as *Letter to Lord North* (1793). It reveals Francis' basic disagreements with Hastings. Indian lands, he felt, should be restored to hereditary owners; revenues payable to the East India Company, as the ruling power, by Indian zemindars should be fixed at a certain sum (and not raised, as done by Hastings, when stockholders demanded more revenue); and that sum should be determined by the capacity of the people and the needs of the government.

Francis was pessimistic about Hastings' regime over Bengal: "A new principle must be assumed for the government of the country, or it must fall."[2] He was bothered by the dual role of the company — as trader and government — and believed that reverting to Indian institutions was preferable to establishing English institutions: "My wish is to revert, as nearly as possible, to the ancient institutions of the country, which, however perverted by the occasional violence of an arbitrary Government, or corrupted by abuses, will, I believe, be found judicious in themselves, and better accommodated to the genius of the people, than any system forcibly introduced from the other side of the globe.''[3] But he was nonetheless a businessman: "We provide for our *interests* when we consult the happiness and prosperity of the people who labour for us.''[4] Francis does not solve the humanitarian issue about English involvement in India, but he is among the earliest to speak out about it.

Francis' moral zeal, like Junius', fused with personal animosity. With a majority of the council following him, Francis was able to overrule Hastings for a while, but when Monson died in 1776, the Francis faction became the minority. Hastings proceeded to eject Francis' appointees and refashion policy. Eventually, however, they reached a compromise: Hastings reinstated two of Francis' protégés, Francis agreed to let Hastings pursue the Mahratta war, and they combined to oppose Impey's judicial pretensions. The agreement did not last long. Hastings officially pronounced Francis "void of truth and honour," which led to a duel (Francis received a severe wound) and to the departure of Francis to England.

Once home, Francis joined with Burke, Fox, Sheridan, and others to participate in the grand event of the 1780s — the impeachment of Hastings. In Parliament and in print, Francis attacked Hastings as a criminal. His *Observations on the Defence Made by Warren Hastings* is an extended, passionate appraisal of Hastings' involvement in the Rohilla war — his bargain with Sujah Dowla, his allowing English troops to be used as mercenaries, their defeat and massacre of the Rohillas, the cruelties practiced by Sujah Dowla under the protection of English troops, and Hastings' attempted defense of the war. "The destruction of a whole people is a felony of the highest order," Francis wrote. "All the accomplices in it are principals. Mr. Hastings was, in every sense that constitutes guilt, a principal in the Rohilla war. He, and he alone, put that sword into the hand of Sujah Dowla, under which the Rohilla nation fell.''[5]

Francis' credit was very high with the forces for impeachment. He supplied Burke with much of the information that formed the charges against Hastings and was nominated by Fox to serve as one of the "managers," that is, prosecutors, in the impeachment. Before Commons rejected the nomination, on the grounds that the duel suggested an inappropriate personal antagonism, Francis delivered a powerful speech, which was immediately published, reviewing his connections with Hastings ("We went to India prejudiced — passionately prejudiced in his favour"),⁶ defending his own conduct, and professing no desire to be engaged in the impeachment. He did, however, argue that the duel should provide no obstacle to his testifying against Hastings: he had consulted with an expert on the subject — "there could not be a stricter and more scrupulous judge of points of honour than he was" — to determine the propriety. The expert was none other than Sir William Draper, the unfortunate victim of Junius' pen a decade earlier.

II   *Francis as Pamphleteer*

Presumably not knowing that Francis was also Junius, Burke pronounced him "the first pamphlet-writer of the age."⁷ An examination of Francis' pamphlets provides abundant evidence for this high praise. If we cannot agree that they are the finest of their age, it is only because they fall short in imagination and wisdom of Burke's own pamphlets. But for clarity, even when dealing with complex issues, for sustained interest, and for spareness of style, Francis' political writings must be ranked very high. Macaulay, who thought highly of Junius, considered Francis' pamphlets to be of the same caliber.

During the 1790s, as Hastings' impeachment dragged on, the dominant intellectual and political issue was the French Revolution and its manifestations in England. An increasingly large number of Englishmen followed Burke's example of opposition to the Revolution, so eloquently argued in his *Reflections on the Revolution in France* (1790), but others felt the spirit of change in the air and attempted to promote it in spite of the growing fanaticism in France and the English-French war. The intellectual differences were fundamental, and long-standing friendships often ended in impassioned argument. Francis sided with the reformers and became one of their most valued spokesmen. In 1792 a group of wealthy Whigs and members of Parliament formed a society called "The Friends of the People," intended to promote moderate, popular reforms. An index of the passions at the time may be seen in the king's reaction to the society, expressed in a letter to Pitt: "The most daring outrage to a regular Government committed by the new Society, who yesterday published its manifesto in several of the newspapers, could only be equalled by some of its leaders standing forth the same day to avow their similar sentiments in the House of Commons. .... If men are to be found willing to overturn the Constitution of this country, it is most providential they so early cast off the mask."[8]

The "Friends" were by no means democrats; notice that their name implies that they — with their wealth, titles, and parliamentary power — were not themselves part of "the people." But their aim was a genuine constitutional reform to give the English people greater representation in government. "What we want is a free House of Commons, and a real representation." Francis wrote the society's *Plan of a Reform,* proposing an end to borough selling, a substantial increase in the number of electors (to prevent the corruption of selling places), and more frequent parliamentary elections. Far from advocating universal manhood suffrage, the society believed that the right to vote should be limited to property owners who pay parish taxes, but, whatever the qualification, it ought to be "so moderate ... that there may be no condition of life in which it may not be acquired by labour, by industry, or by talents." "Understood in this sense," Francis wrote, "the representation in Parliament would be really and substantially universal."[9] The plan was circulated and debated in Parliament, but nothing came of it. The reaction against the Revolution stifled most pleas for reform until long after Francis' death, but the minority voice of reformers provided an important service in the long run. "The adherence of the Whigs to Parliamentary Reform in days when it was impracticable," Trevelyan maintained, "enabled them, when the wheel had come full circle, to avert civil war and social catastrophe by their Reform Bill of 1832."[10]

Francis covered a wide range of material in his political writing. Besides his reform pamphlets, he wrote a substantial paper on financial affairs, *Reflections on the Abundance of Paper in Circulation and the Scarcity of Specie* (1810), arguing that through an imbalance of trade, gold and silver were flowing out of the country, that property holders were severely overtaxed, and that the increasing paper circulation was dangerously lacking in security. The self-consciously immoderate *Letter to Earl Grey* (1814), unlike the *Plan of a Reform,* shows signs of the old Junian irony in Francis' scornful attack on England's "zeal in the cause of morality and religion" while invading "defenseless, neutral" Denmark and imposing a blockade on Norway.[11] And his last pamphlet, *Historical Questions Exhibited,* is a quasi-satirical enquiry into the legitimacy of royal families. It is filled with invective, sneers, attacks on the Stuarts, the French, the Scots, David Hume, the fat, ugly mistresses of George I, and a host of other historical and contemporary objects that crossed the view of the seventy-eight-year-old pamphleteer.

One of Francis' best, and most characteristic, pamphlets, is a short work, *On the Regency.* In November, 1810, the death of Princess Amelia, George III's youngest daughter and favorite child, led to a recurrence of the king's supposed madness. Since he was totally incapable of business and his physicians were not optimistic about recovery, the ministry introduced a Recency Bill which would give the Prince of Wales the title of regent but restrict his executive powers considerably. The ostensible reason for the bill was that the king might recover and resume his duties at any time; the unspoken reason was that the Prince of Wales was friendly to the Whig opposition, including Francis, and was expected to overturn the present ministry totally if he had the power.

Francis was naturally a strong partisan on the issue; he believed the regent should have the full powers of a king. But in his pamphlet he speaks as a noble, disinterested defender of the constitution and, like Chatham, whose ghost is invoked at the beginning and end, as the preserver of freedom. "I speak to the nation, and not for any interest of my own," he says, and appends a Junian sentiment of martyrdom if the nation should fail to heed him. He argues the constitutional issue in clear, cogent language, and scorns the abstract for the practical in defending the hereditary succession to the crown: "All other magistrates are chosen for their merits or qualifications. The office of the chief magistrate alone is too great an object of ambition to be left open to a contest. In the abstract idea of election, one may see a possibility that the best would be chosen. But it is vain to talk of theories, with the example of Poland before us."[12] Like Junius, Francis scorns authority, threatens the power of the people without condoning it, and apparently demolishes his antagonists' position with a climactic succession of rhetorical questions ("Junius asks questions incomparably well," Coleridge had noted).[13]

The pamphlet is passionate and convincing, yet it is remarkable that Francis, using many of the former Junian devices and sentiments, is employing them for apparently antithetical purposes. The explanation serves to display the slipperiness of the politics and pamphlet warfare of the time. Francis was no more disinterested and aloof in this case than Junius or Veteran were in theirs; under the surface of this argument lie Francis' personal friendship and political alliance with the Prince of Wales and his political antagonism to the ministry. As it happened, however, Francis' cause was no more successful than Junius'. The Regency Bill passed, giving the regent limited and eventually full executive power, but on gaining his power the regent discarded his Whig friends and cast his lot with his father's ministers.

III   *Parliamentary Issues*

As a member of the House of Commons for eighteen years, Francis spoke on many occasions in parliamentary debates; most of these speeches are recorded and may be examined in the records of the House. His most important speeches, however, were also published as pamphlets for broader dissemination. A number of speeches on Indian affairs as well as others on parliamentary reform, economics, military affairs, and slavery found their way into print.

In some of his published speeches, Francis displays a brilliance not unlike that found in the Junius letters, but the brilliance is adapted to the public arena. In the debate on Grey's motion for a reform of the election procedures in Parliament, the chief spokesman in opposition to the motion was William Windham, a former ally of Francis'. Francis delivered and published a speech favoring reform which consisted of a satiric character of Windham and an attack on his arguments.

Since the speech is that of Philip Francis and not some anonymous scribbler, the tactics differed from Junius', but the result is similar. In it, Francis pretends that he is not attacking his "right honourable friend" but only soliciting "an amicable discussion."[14] He ironically denigrates himself as a man of no imagination or eloquence, then with elaborately witty metaphors describes Windham's speech as one which soars and dives but never lands on "plain level ground" to consider a "plain terrestial question" of reform. A witty character of Windham evolves: he is noble, eloquent, and brilliant, with the "preternatural activity of mind" that one finds in a madman; he suffers from monomania about the French Revolution ("The French revolution is an answer to everything; the French revolution is his everlasting theme, the universal remedy, the never-failing panacea, the perpetual burthen of his song; ... a cold, flat, insipid hash of the same dish, perpetually

served up to us in different shapes"), and, above all, he is the metaphysician who accuses everyone else of being a metaphysician.
"The House have heard him, with every pleasure that belongs to
astonishment, while he ranged over the whole circuit of human
science, and glided through every region of the moral as well as the
intellectual world; through ethics, mechanics, pneumatics,
hydraulics, geography, mathematics, astronomy, and logic;
through all the polite arts, of swimming, flying, burning, skaiting,
diving; the learning of his library, and the meditations of his closet.
On one subject alone he has studiously maintained a most delicate
reserve" — parliamentary reform. With the same Junian playful-
ness with words, the same malice seasoned with wit, the same
gusto, Francis is back to his former activity — personal attack for
political ends — but without the incognito.

His three speeches published as *Proceedings in the House of
Commons on the Slave Trade* (1796), however, shun wit for passion. They are among his most moving writings, revealing his
strongest humanitarian impulses, his most impassioned prose, and
his most fundamental principles. The English had established a
thriving commercial triangle, sending English manufactures to
Africa, African slaves to the West Indies, and West Indian sugar
back to England. William Wilberforce led the attempt to abolish
slave trade, and he was supported by such men as Pitt, Grenville,
and Fox, but in the 1790s no reform movement was able to counter
the revolutionary reaction. Nevertheless, Francis devoted himself
completely to the cause.

The arguments against abolition of the slave trade were chiefly
commercial. Alderman Sawbridge, the radical London politician,
did not favor abolition because, he said, tampering with the slave
trade would ruin London. In the parliamentary debates, Francis
heard other objections: abolition would be a disservice to present
slaves by encouraging rebellion; it would ruin English estates in the
West Indies (some of them owned by members of Parliament); it
would violate the "justice and humanity" due to the proprietors of
West Indian lands; it would "terminate all spirit of adventure, all
incitement to industry, all thirst of emulation."[15] Francis heard the
objections with indignation. On no other issue did he commit himself so thoroughly to an argument on principle: "Many gentlemen,
indeed, have asserted what they have by no means established, and
what upon the whole, I utterly disbelieve, that this trade is
unprofitable; but no man has yet had the courage to affirm, or even

to insinuate, that it is not criminal."[16] Whatever the consequences of abolition, whether loss of money, or loss of colonies, they should be met. To the landowners, he enjoined: "Do justice before you demand it."

Francis stood to lose a substantial inheritance by speaking for abolition, but he spoke anyway, and did lose the inheritance.[17] In 1796 he immersed himself in research on the subject — the evils involved in the slave trade, the commercial repercussions of abolition, and the means by which slavery could be terminated. On April 11 he delivered his conclusions to Parliament and offered a "Bill for the better Regulation and Improvement of the State and Condition of the Negro and other Slaves." His program, dealing with slaves already in the West Indies, was an elaborate one: slaves should be paid, from which they should be allowed to buy their freedom; they should be given small plots of land, which could not be taken away; they should be encouraged to marry; they should have their own juries for trying Negroes; and they should not be converted by well-meaning Christians. But the scheme failed to gain a majority, just as his impassioned portrayal of the whipping of slaves had failed to gain a majority for Wilberforce's motion. By 1807, however, there was enough support in Parliament to abolish the slave trade; the abolition of slavery itself came still later.

IV *Francis and Burke*

Francis met Edmund Burke in 1773, before going to India. Once there he corresponded with Burke occasionally, but it was not until Francis returned to England in 1781 that they became close friends. Their friendship is not surprising, for they had much in common. Both were members of Parliament, both Whigs in opposition to the ministry, both men of extensive political experience, and both excellent writers — one being suspected as author of the Junius letters and the other being the unsuspected actual author. Above all, both were ardently opposed to the course of affairs in India, and especially to Warren Hastings. Burke became the parliamentary leader of the Hastings impeachment, and Francis became the primary source of information. On the occasion of their disagreement in 1790, Burke wrote to Francis, "I do not recollect since I first had the pleasure of your acquaintance that there has been an heat or a coolness of a single days duration on my side during the whole time."[18] Yet Francis was never a man with whom such an unruffled friendship was easy; though his affection, as well as his malice, was strong, he was outspoken, temperamental, and even rude (to no less than the Prince of Wales). Francis told Burke, probably correctly, that "I am the only friend ... who ever ventures to contradict or oppose you, face to face, on subjects of this nature [that is, the revolution in France]."[19]

It is significant to Francis' reputation as a writer that Burke — considered by some to be one of the great stylists of the English language — should often demur to Francis on matters of style. Francis noted that at Burke's own desire he had "corrected the whole" of many of Burke's India papers — "I mean in minor particulars and lapses of expression; all which he left at my disposal, not only in these reports but in many of his speeches and other writings."[20] When Burke was composing his *magnum opus, Reflections on the Revolution in France,* he showed his drafts to only four friends — Sir Joshua Reynolds, William Windham, Sir Gilbert Eliot, and Francis.

Francis did not admire anything that he found in the *Reflections* — not the style, the arrangement, the "general tendency," or the substance. "Once for all, I wish you would let me teach you to write English. To me, who am to read everything you write, it would be great comfort, and to you no sort of disparagement. Why will you not allow yourself to be persuaded, that polish is material to preservation?"[21] It was, Francis told Burke after reading the draft, "very loosely put together"; it contained too much "jest and sneer and sarcasm" when it should be "grave, direct, and serious"; and the famous passage on Marie Antoinette and chivalry, Francis proclaimed "pure foppery."[22]

The French Revolution was the great dividing issue of the 1790s; it split many friendships, including that between Burke and Francis. Despite their similarities and their immense respect for each other, the fundamental issues raised by the French Revolution — about the value of history, the nature of political institutions, and human morality — acted as a wedge which drove the two increasingly apart. Burke forbade any further discussion of the Revolution — "Therefore let us end here all discussion on the subject"[23] — and although they continued to collaborate on the impeachment, they did so coolly. In his long speech on West Indian slave trade, published the year before Burke died, Francis paid homage to his acknowledged superior, with whom he was to have no further contact: "Divided, as we are, by an irreconcileable dif-

ference of opinion on another important subject, and separated in
private life as long as that unfortunate question continues, I still
hope and believe that the bond of personal friendship and goodwill between us will never be dissolved. . . . On a transcendent question, such as this, of morals implicated with policy, the eminence of
[Burke's] mind extends his view, and gives him an horizon, which
vulgar vision cannot reach to."[24]

Burke's mind and achievement, in the final analysis, far excel
Francis', but the personal, literary, and political connections between them add considerable luster to Francis' career.

CHAPTER 9

Conclusion

I like him; — he was a good hater." Byron meant this to be a compliment,[1] and he is right: Junius *was* a good hater. But there have been many good haters who lacked the literary talent of Junius, and it should be added that Junius' malice was not pure. Controlled hatred is the natural emotion for good political invective, and therefore the most important one for Junius, but the letters convey, above all, a sense of Junius as a man of strong feelings — malicious and otherwise. "He who feels deeply, will express strongly," Francis wrote, many years after Junius.[2] The importance of human feelings in political thought and writing, the importance of the "heart," is a theme that runs throughout the Junius letters. Because his writing was inspired by opposition to the government and the state of England, the theme took a distinctly pessimistic bent, but the letters are by no means the product of a warped mind.

Junius was obsessed by what he called "spirit." He was always looking — in vain — for a "man of spirit" to lead the nation, a Chatham restored to health and power. Grafton had none, George III had none; as men, they fell short even of the despised Cromwell: "But, with all his crimes, [Cromwell] had the spirit of an Englishman" (p. 226). The English people, however, had spirit and could be roused to exert it, which was the weapon Junius held over the king and ministry. And, of course, Junius possessed it. "Spirit" rather than hatred is the distinguishing quality of his writings; it is felt in the vigor of his prose, the warmth of his feelings, and the confident assertion of his rightness.

As an original thinker, Junius has no claim to greatness; his forte is the uncommon expression of commonplace sentiments.[3] He followed Grenville's ideas in the *Present State of the Nation* very closely for a while, and when something better came along — as it did in Burke's *Thoughts on the Cause of the Present Discontents* —

he dropped the old ideas and adopted the new. (Burke's cast of mind and his sentiments, however, struck a genuinely responsive chord with Junius: "Would to God it were true," Burke wrote, "that the fault of our peers was too much spirit.")[4] But although not original, Junius was no mere parasite. He had his own vision of political disintegration, and he availed himself of whatever ideas became current in order to convey that vision with as much clarity and force as possible. With his literary talent he applied ideas to the world of experience in a way that had lasting effect. As Harold J. Laski said, "He won a new audience for political conflict and that audience was the unfranchised populace of England. His letters, moreover, appearing as they did in the daily journals gave the press a significance in politics which it never lost."[5]

The *Letters of Junius* is at once a literary work and an event in history. We see Grafton in the letters not as a historical object but as a person living among, and trying to govern, other people, and doing it badly enough to provoke the malice and wit of Junius. Perceiving Grafton through Junius, and doing so with some knowledge of Grafton and his time, provides an imaginative understanding of the period impossible otherwise. Such an understanding requires seeing Junius in his literary tradition — the peculiar blend of a Johnsonian literature of experience and Augustan satire. Of this kind of writing Junius is undoubtedly the best. "As for Junius," Hazlitt said, "he is at the head of his class; but," he rightly added, "that class is not the highest."[6]

It is sometimes said that without the mystery of Junius' identity, he would not have been remembered after the 1770s. This is indeed possible, given the innate transitoriness of political letters; nearly all other political letters, anonymous and otherwise, have long been forgotten. But then Junius without his mystery is inconceivable: mystery was an integral part of his rhetorical character. When Junius appeared at the bar of Heaven, in Byron's *Vision of Judgment,* to testify as witness on whether George III should be allowed entrance, even the Archangel was awestruck and baffled:

> The shadow came — a tall, thin, grey-hair'd figure,
>   That look'd as it had been a shade on earth;
> Quick in its motions, with an air of vigour,
>   But nought to mark its breeding or its birth;
> Now it wax'd little, then again grew bigger,
>   With now an air of gloom, or savage mirth;

> But as you gazed upon its features, they
> Changed every instant — to *what,* none could say.[7]

And Junius, *qua* Junius, the rhetorical creation, remains a shadow today though we are more confident about the facts of his creation than Byron was. (Byron's jocular solution was that Junius was *"really, truly,* nobody at all": letters and books have been written without heads, so there is no reason why letters may not be written without hands!)

The fact is that Junius as a political and literary phenomenon fares remarkably well two centuries after his battles had been fought. In recent years, Alvar Ellegard has established the Junian canon and confirmed his identity, the historian A. W. Rowse has written a spirited appreciation of him, James Boulton has brilliantly analyzed his literary qualities, and John Cannon has ably edited his works. The most appropriate twentieth-century attitude has probably been expressed by Louis Bredvold, Robert Root, and George Sherburn, who, unconcerned about the fact of identity, have focussed on the fact of the letters themselves and their peculiar power: "His letters bravely championed the cause of English liberty and of the English constitution. He was distinguished for moral courage as well as for skill in fiery denunciation; a noble purpose redeems what would otherwise be mere personalities, and every reader who lingers long over the *Letters* must come at last to feel an admiration akin to awe for this mysterious lonely figure who achieved one of the greatest feats in the history of political journalism."[8]

Notes and References

Preface

1. W. E. H. Lecky, *A History of England in the Eighteenth Century,*
III (New York: Appleton, 1888), 267.

Chapter One

1. James Routledge, *Chapters in the History of Popular Progress*
(London: Macmillan, 1876), p. 148.
2. *Coleridge's Miscellaneous Criticism,* ed. T. M. Raysor (Cambridge:
Harvard University Press, 1936), p. 314.
3. See James T. Boulton, *The Language of Politics in the Age of
Wilkes and Burke* (London: Routledge & Kegan Paul, 1963), pp. 21,
24–25, 31.
4. *The Augustans,* ed. Maynard Mack (New York: Prentice-Hall,
1950), p. 32.
5. *Horace Walpole's Correspondence with Sir Horace Mann,* ed. W.
S. Lewis et al., VI (New Haven: Yale University Press, 1960), 169.
6. For a brief survey of eighteenth-century London daily newspapers,
see the introduction to Lucyle Werkmeister, *The London Daily Press,
1772–1792* (Lincoln: University of Nebraska Press, 1963).
7. *Idler,* No. 7, in *The Idler and The Adventurer,* ed. W. J. Bate et al.
(New Haven: Yale University Press, 1963), p. 22.
8. John Lord Campbell, *The Lives of the Lord Chancellors,* VI
(London: John Murray, 1847), 347 n.
9. Ibid., 347.
10. *The Grenville Papers,* ed. W. J. Smith, IV (London: John Murray,
1853), 425 n.

Chapter Two

1. *The Letters of Junius,* ed. John Cannon (Oxford: Clarendon Press,
1978), p. 8. Hereafter cited in the text by page number. When quoting
from the private correspondence, I have spelled out Junius' abbreviations.
2. The epigraph *Stat Nominis Umbra* Junius adapted from Lucan's
Pharsalia, I, 135. Junius probably took his name from Marcus Junius
Brutus, the assassin of Caesar.
3. *Boswell's Life of Samuel Johnson,* ed. G. B. Hill and L. F. Powell,

III (Oxford: Clarendon Press, 1934), 376, n.

4. Ibid.

5. C. W. Dilke, *The Papers of a Critic* (London: John Murray, 1875), pp. 14, 16.

6. Reprinted by Taylor in *The Identity of Junius with a Distinguished Living Character Established* (London: Taylor and Hessey, 1816), p. 20.

7. Joseph Parkes and Herman Merivale, *Memoirs of Sir Philip Francis* (London: Longmans, Green, 1867), I, 324–25. Hereafter cited as *Memoirs*.

8. Taylor, p. 354.

9. Speech in Parliament, February 12, 1787; Taylor, p. 97.

10. Campbell, VI, 344–47.

11. Thomas DeQuincey, *New Essays,* ed. Stuart M. Tave (Princeton University Press, 1966), p. 259.

12. H. R. Francis, *Junius Revealed* (London: Longmans, Green, 1894), p. 53.

13. Charles Chabot, *The Handwriting of Junius Professionally Investigated* (London: John Murray, 1871); Leslie Stephen, "Chatham, Francis, and Junius," *English Historical Review,* 3 (1888), 233–49.

14. See Francesco Cordasco, *A Junius Bibliography,* rev. ed. (New York: Burt Franklin, 1974), entries 258, 260, 331, 338, 341, 342. For a review of Cramp, see Dilke, pp. 140–52.

15. *The Authorship of the Letters of Junius Elucidated* (London: J. R. Smith, 1848), p. vii.

16. Wednesday, January 2. Quoted in DeQuincey's *New Essays,* p. 260.

17. *The Grenville Papers,* IV, ccxxviii.

18. James Smith, *Junius Unveiled* (London: Dent, 1909), p. 56.

19. William H. Graves, *Junius Finally Discovered* (Birmingham, Ala.: Dispatch Printing Co., 1917).

20. *The Nation and Athenaeum,* 42 (February 4, 1928), 688.

21. *Who Was Junius?* (Stockholm: Almqvist & Wiksell, 1962), p. 108.

22. Ibid., p. 118. Ellegard provides a detailed explanation of his method in *A Statistical Method for Determining Authorship: the Junius Letters, 1769–72,* Gothenburg Studies in English, No. 13 (Stockholm: Almqvist & Wiksell, 1962).

23. The most recent editor, John Cannon, concludes that Junius was Francis. For an able survey of the issue, see "A Note on Authorship" in his *Letters of Junius,* pp. 537–72. New evidence supporting Francis was presented in L. S. Sutherland, W. Doyle, J. M. J. Rogister, "Junius and Philip Francis: New Evidence," *Bulletin of the Institute of Historical Research,* 42 (1969), 158–72. Professor Cordasco has claimed since 1949 to have documents proving that Junius was Lauchlin Macleane but, nearly thirty years later, has not shown them to anyone. For the as yet weak case for Macleane, see the introduction to Cordasco's *Junius Bibliography* and

James N. M. Maclean, *Reward is Secondary* (London: Hodder and Stoughton, 1963).

Chapter Three

1. *Gibbon's Journal,* ed. D. M. Low (New York: W. W. Norton, 1929), p. 145.
2. *The North Briton,* No. 45, is reprinted in *Political Writers of Eighteenth-Century England,* ed. Jeffrey Hart (New York: Knopf, 1964), pp. 259–64.
3. Quoted by George Nobbe, *The North Briton: A Study in Political Propaganda* (New York: Columbia University Press, 1939), pp. 230–31.
4. *Junius,* ed. John Wade (London: Bohn, 1850), II, 164–65. Hereafter cited in the text as Wade, with volume and page number. For attributions of miscellaneous letters to Junius, see Ellegard, *Who Was Junius,* chapter 7, and Cannon, *The Letters of Junius,* appendix 5. I have followed Ellegard's conclusions on the Junian canon.
5. Edmund Burke, *Thoughts on the Cause of the Present Discontents,* in *Works* (Boston: Little, Brown, 1880), I, 437.
6. *The False Alarm,* in *Political Writings,* ed. Donald J. Greene (New Haven: Yale University Press, 1977), p. 345.
7. Ibid., 319.
8. *Memoirs,* I, 261.
9. Ibid., p. 262.
10. Ibid., p. 264.

Chapter Four

1. Quoted in *Junius,* ed. Wade, I, 4.
2. *The Present State of the Nation* (London: J. Almon, 1768), p. 32.
3. Lecky, III, 15.
4. For a more elaborate account of these three theories concerning the accession of George III, see Dorothy Marshall, *Eighteenth Century England* (London: Longmans, 1962), pp. 322–28, and Herbert Butterfield, *George III and the Historians* (London: Collins, 1957), pp. 41–295. For Namier's argument, see his *Structure of Politics at the Accession of George III,* 2 vols. (London: Macmillan, 1929).
5. Burke, I, 441.
6. Ibid., 469.
7. Ibid.
8. The establishment of parties and the history of this period are brilliantly analyzed by Harvey C. Mansfield, Jr., in *Statesmanship and Party Government* (Chicago: University of Chicago Press, 1965).
9. Burke, I, 447.

10. Ibid., 468.

11. Ibid., 466; italics added. See Mansfield, pp. 36–39.

12. Burke, I, 444–47; Mansfield, p. 31.

13. Lecky, III, 168.

14. *Dictionary of National Biography* (1921–22), VII, 199.

15. *Memoirs,* I, 250.

16. Ibid.

17. *Thoughts on the Late Transactions Respecting Falkland's Islands,* in *Political Writings,* p. 371.

18. *Memoirs,* I, 253.

19. *Political Writings,* pp. 379, 384.

20. Quoted in Wade's *Junius,* II, 342.

Chapter Five

1. David Hume, "Of the Liberty of the Press," in *Essays Moral, Political and Literary* (London: Oxford University Press, 1963), p. 8.

2. Ibid., p. 12.

3. Edward Perritt, "The Government and the Newspaper Press in England," *Political Science Quarterly,* 12 (1897), 669.

4. See Fredrick S. Siebert, *Freedom of the Press in England, 1476–1776* (Urbana: University of Illinois Press, 1952), pp. 305–92.

5. Jean Louis DeLolme, *The Constitution of England,* ed. John MacGregor (London: Bohn, 1853), p. 50. Originally published 1770.

6. Werkmeister, p. 7.

7. Boswell's *Life,* I, 394; "Milton," in *Lives of the English Poets,* ed. G. B. Hill (Oxford: Clarendon Press, 1905), I, 108.

8. See H. M. Lubasz, "Public Opinion Comes of Age," *History Today,* 8 (1958), 453–61.

9. Quoted in Robert R. Rea, *The English Press in Politics, 1760–1774* (Lincoln: University of Nebraska Press, 1963), p. 178.

10. Ibid., pp. 183–84.

11. Leslie Stephen, "Chatham, Francis, and Junius," *English Historical Review,* 3 (1888), 233–49.

Chapter Six

1. *Falkland's Islands,* in *Political Writings,* p. 378.

2. Basil Williams, *The Whig Supremacy, 1714–1760,* 2d ed., rev. C. H. Stuart (Oxford: Clarendon Press, 1962), p. 30.

3. Lecky, III, 188.

4. DeLolme, p. 219.

5. *The False Alarm,* in *Political Writings,* p. 344.

6. Quoted in Lecky, III, 21, 111.

7. DeLolme, p. xx.

8. Boswell's *Life,* IV, 117.

9. Richard Pares, *King George III and the Politicians* (Oxford: Clarendon Press, 1953), p. 72.

10. Burke, I, 530. See Mansfield, pp. 17–19.

Chapter Seven

1. Boswell's *Life,* III, 376.

2. Ed. A. W. Ward and A. R. Waller (Cambridge: Cambridge University Press, 1952), X, 405–6. Originally published 1913.

3. *Johnson's England,* ed. A. S. Turberville (Oxford: Clarendon Press, 1933), II, 351.

4. *The Complete Works of William Hazlitt,* ed. P. P. Howe, XVII (London: Dent, 1933), 64.

5. *A History of Eighteenth Century Literature* (London: Macmillan, 1891), pp. 363–64.

6. Thomas DeQuincey, *Selected Essays on Rhetoric,* ed. Frederick Burwick (Carbondale: Southern Illinois University Press, 1967), p. 119.

7. See Edmund Burke, *A Philosophical Enquiry into . . . the Sublime and Beautiful,* ed. J. T. Boulton (Notre Dame, Ind.: University of Notre Dame Press, 1968), p. 80.

8. *Coleridge's Miscellaneous Criticism,* p. 314.

9. *Public Advertiser,* August 22, 1771. Quoted in Wade's *Junius,* I, 50.

10. *Coleridge's Miscellaneous Criticism,* p. 317.

11. The best treatment of Junius' literary qualities is James T. Boulton, *The Language of Politics* (London: Routledge & Kegan Paul, 1963), pp. 16–31. Boulton finds Junius "quite securely in the Augustan tradition of satire" (p. 31).

12. *Coleridge's Miscellaneous Criticism,* pp. 317–18. For a different interpretation of Junius' use of character, see Richard Sennett, *The Fall of Public Man* (New York: Knopf, 1977), p. 104.

13. *MacFlecknoe,* lines 17–20.

14. *New Essays,* p. 267 n.

15. Quoted in Wade's *Junius,* I, 4.

16. *Coleridge's Miscellaneous Criticism,* p. 319.

Chapter Eight

1. *The Correspondence of Edmund Burke,* ed. Thomas W. Copeland et al., III (Cambridge: Cambridge University Press, 1961), 402–3.

2. *Letter from Mr. Francis to Lord North* (London: J. Debrett, [1793]), p. 56.

3. Ibid., pp. 43–44.

4. Ibid., p. 10.

5. (London: J. Debrett, 1787), p. 44.

6. Quoted from *The Parliamentary History of England* (London: Hansard, 1815), XXVI, 1327.

7. Taylor, p. 98.

8. *The Later Correspondence of George III,* ed. A. Aspinall, I (Cambridge: Cambridge University Press, 1962), 591.

9. *Plan of a Reform in the Election of the House of Commons* (London: Ridgway, 1817), pp. 20, 24.

10. G. M. Trevelyan, *History of England* (Garden City, N.Y.: Doubleday, 1952), III, 93. Originally published 1926.

11. *Letter from Sir Philip Francis . . . to Earl Grey* (London: Ridgway, 1814), pp. 5, 9–10, 12.

12. Reprinted in Taylor, pp. 216–19.

13. *Coleridge's Miscellaneous Criticism,* p. 317.

14. *Parliamentary History,* XXX, 840–49.

15. Ibid., XXXII, 866–67.

16. Ibid., XXIX, 287.

17. See Ibid., XXXII, 809. Francis was to have inherited a sizeable property in the West Indies from a close friend of the family. When he persisted in opposing slavery in the face of her "earnest and repeated solicitations," she changed her benefactor.

18. *Correspondence of Burke,* VI, 88.

19. Ibid., VI, 85.

20. *Memoirs,* II, 287.

21. *Correspondence of Burke,* VI, 151.

22. Ibid., VI, 86.

23. Ibid., VI, 173.

24. *Parliamentary History,* XXXII, 968–69.

Chapter Nine

1. *Byron's Letters and Journals,* ed. Leslie A. Marchand, III (Cambridge: Harvard University Press, 1974), 215.

2. *Reflections on the Abundance of Paper in Circulation* (London: Ridgway, 1810), p. 44.

3. See *Coleridge's Miscellaneous Prose,* pp. 220, 314.

4. *Thoughts on the . . . Present Discontents,* in *Works,* I, 458.

5. *Political Thought in England from Locke to Bentham* (New York: Holt, 1920), p. 220.

6. *Complete Works,* VII, 313.

7. Stanza 75.

8. *Eighteenth Century Prose* (New York: Ronald Press, 1932), p. 850.

Selected Bibliography

PRIMARY SOURCES

1. Editions of Junius' Writings

The Letters of Junius ... with Notes and Illustrations, Historical, Political, Biographical, and Critical. 2 vols. Edited by Robert Heron. London: Harrison, 1802. Intelligent and valuable commentary on each letter of the 1772 edition.

Junius: Including Letters by the Same Writer under Other Signatures (Now First Collected). 3 vols. [Edited by J. Mason Good.] London: Woodfall, 1812. Includes the 1772 text, plus Junius' private correspondence to Wilkes and Woodfall, and "miscellaneous letters" of Junius (many incorrectly attributed). For more accurate attributions, see Ellegard, *Who Was Junius?,* chapter 7, and the Cannon edition, appendix 5.

Junius: Including Letters by the Same Writer under Other Signatures. 2 vols. Edited by John Wade. London: Bohn, 1850. Reprints Mason Good's 1812 edition, to which Wade added an introductory essay and extensive notes. Attacked by Dilke, *Papers of a Critic.* The best edition for the miscellaneous letters not printed in the Cannon edition.

The Letters of Junius. Edited by C. W. Everett. London: Faber & Gwyer, 1927. Reviewed by Lewis B. Namier, *The Nation and Athenaeum,* 42 (February 4, 1928), 688.

The Letters of Junius. Edited by John Cannon. Oxford: Clarendon Press, 1978. The standard edition. Includes Junius' public and private letters and some (but not all) of the miscellaneous letters under other signatures.

2. Philip Francis' Writings

Original Minutes ... on the Settlement and Collection of the Revenues of Bengal. London: J. Debrett, 1782. Written in 1776.

Speech in the House of Commons on Friday, July 2, 1784. London: J. Debrett, 1784. On affairs of the East India Company.

Two Speeches in the House of Commons on the Original East-India Bill and on the Amended Bill on the 16th and 26th of July, 1784. London: J. Debrett, 1784.

Observations on the Defence Made by Warren Hastings. London: J. Debrett, 1787.

House of Commons, Tuesday, 11th December, 1787. London: n.p., 1787. A publication of Francis' speech prior to his being rejected as a manager of the Hastings' impeachment.

Answer of Philip Francis, Esq. to the Charge Brought Against Sir John Clavering, Colonel George Monson, and Mr. Francis . . . by Sir Elijah Impey. London: J. Jarvis, 1788.

Letter from Mr. Francis to Lord North. London: J. Debrett, [1793]. On Indian affairs; written in 1777.

Speech of Philip Francis . . . in the House of Commons, on Friday, February 26, 1796. London: J. Debrett, 1796. On public loans.

Proceedings in the House of Commons on the Slave Trade. London: Ridgway, 1796. Contains three of Francis' parliamentary speeches.

The Question as It Stood in March, 1798. London, 1798.

Mr. Francis's Speech on the Affairs of India: Delivered in the House of Commons, on the 29 of July, 1803. London: E. Harding, 1803.

Speeches in the House of Commons on the War against the Mahrattas. London: J. Ridgway, 1805.

Mr. Francis's Speech in the House of Commons . . . 28 of May, 1806, against the Exemption of Foreign Property, in the Funds from the Duty on Income. London: Ridgway, 1806.

A Letter from Sir Philip Francis . . . to Lord Viscount Howick, on the State of the East India Company. 2d ed. London: J. Ridgway, 1807.

On the Regency. London: Harding and Wright, 1810. Reprinted in Taylor, *The Identity of Junius,* pp. 216–23.

Reflections on the Abundance of Paper in Circulation and the Scarcity of Specie. London: Ridgway, 1810.

Letter from Sir Philip Francis . . . to Earl Grey. London: Ridgway, 1814. On the English blockade of Norway.

A Letter Missive from Sir Philip Francis, to Lord Holland. London: Ridgway, 1816.

Plan of a Reform in the Election of the House of Commons. London: Ridgway, 1817. Written in 1795 for the "Friends of the People."

Historical Questions Exhibited in the Morning Chronicle. London: J. Ridgway, 1818.

SECONDARY SOURCES

BOULTON, JAMES T. *The Language of Politics in the Age of Wilkes and Burke.* London: Routledge & Kegan Paul, 1963. An excellent discussion of the political literature of Junius and others.

BOWYER, T.H. *A Bibliographical Examination of the Earliest Editions of the Letters of Junius.* Charlottesville: University of Virginia Press, 1957.

BROUGHAM, HENRY LORD. *Historical Sketches of Statesmen Who Flourished in the Time of George III.* 2d ser. London: Charles Knight, 1839. Contains a sketch of Sir Philip Francis' life and character.

CAMPBELL, JOHN LORD. *The Lives of the Lord Chancellors.* 8 vols. London: John Murray, 1845–69. Contains Lady Francis' important but untrustworthy testimony about her husband (VI, 344–47).

Coleridge's Miscellaneous Criticism. Edited by Thomas M. Raysor. Cambridge: Harvard University Press, 1936. Contains Coleridge's marginalia on Junius, pp. 313–19.

CORDASCO, FRANCESCO. *A Junius Bibliography.* Revised edition. New York: Burt Franklin, 1974. The most complete bibliography of Junian studies.

DEQUINCEY, THOMAS. *Collected Writings.* Edited by David Masson. London: Black, 1897. Discussions of Junius in *London Reminiscenses* (III, 132–43), "Rhetoric" (X, 117–20), and "Schlosser's Literary History of the Eighteenth Century" (XI, 41–49).

————. *New Essays.* Edited by Stuart M. Tave. Princeton: Princeton University Press, 1966. Contains DeQuincey's anonymous contributions to the *Edinburgh Post;* an excellent summary of and comment on Taylor's pro-Francis arguments.

DILKE, CHARLES WENTWORTH. *The Papers of a Critic.* London: John Murray, 1875. Skeptical criticism on the identity of Junius; essays originally appeared in the *Athenaeum* between 1848 and 1860.

ELLEGARD, ALVAR. *Who Was Junius?* Stockholm: Almqvist & Wiksell, 1962. The author (Philip Francis) determined by a statistical analysis of style. Also contains a sound, readable survey of quest for Junius. Important review in *Times Literary Supplement,* January 25, 1963, p. 67.

The Francis Letters. 2 vols. Edited by Beata Francis and Eliza Keary. London: Hutchinson, 1900. Less valuable than Parkes and Merivale, *Memoirs.*

The Grenville Papers. 4 vols. Edited by William James Smith. London: John Murray, 1852–53. Smith's essay in volume 3 argues that Richard Grenville, Earl Temple, was Junius; three new Junius letters to George Grenville are in IV, 254, 354, 379.

JOHNSON, SAMUEL. *Thoughts on the Late Transactions Respecting Falkland's Islands.* In *Political Writings,* edited by Donald J. Greene. New Haven: Yale University Press, 1977. A reply to, and attack on, Junius.

LECKY, W. E. H. *A History of England in the Eighteenth Century.* New York: Appleton, 1888–90. Valuable comments on Junius in the context of his age, III, 253–77.

MACAULAY, THOMAS B. "Warren Hastings." In *Critical and Historical Essays*. Boston: Houghton Mifflin, 1900. V, 114–242. Contains a character of Francis, discusses his Indian activities, and argues his claims to the Junius letters.

MACLEAN, JAMES N. M. *Reward is Secondary: The Life of a Political Adventurer and an Inquiry into the Mystery of 'Junius.'* London: Hodder and Stoughton, 1963. Argues the case for Lauchlin Maclean as part of a "Tripartite Junius."

MCCUE, DANIEL L., JR. "Burke and Philip Francis: Revolution versus Friendship." *Burke Newsletter*, 6 (1964–65), 394–99.

PARKES, JOSEPH, and MERIVALE, HERMAN. *Memoirs of Sir Philip Francis with Correspondence and Journals*. 2 vols. London: Longmans, Green, 1867. An invaluable compendium of Francis' life and letters. Untrustworthy in the early years (to 1768).

RAE, W. FRASER. *The Athenaeum*, August 11, 1888, pp. 192–93; August 25, 1888, pp. 258–60; September 8, 1888, pp. 319–21; December 14, 1889, pp. 222–23; June 28, 1890, pp. 831–33. Criticism of various theories about Junius' identity.

REA, ROBERT R. *The English Press in Politics, 1760–1774*. Lincoln: University of Nebraska Press, 1963. Examines in detail the government's reaction to Junius' "Address to the King."

ROWSE, A. L. *The English Spirit*. Rev. ed. New York: Funk & Wagnalls, 1966.

STANHOPE, PHILIP HENRY (LORD MAHON). *History of England from the Peace of Utrecht*. 7 vols. London: John Murray, 1836–54. Presents Junius in his historical context and the claims of Francis (V, 320–41).

STEPHEN, LESLIE. "Chatham, Francis, and Junius." *English Historical Review*, 3 (1888), 233–49. Brilliantly explains the relationship between these three.

STEPHEN, LESLIE. "Sir Philip Francis." *Dictionary of National Biography*. Ed. Leslie Stephen and Sidney Lee. New York: Macmillan, 1908. VII, 611–20. The best short biography of Francis.

SUTHERLAND, L. S., DOYLE, W. and ROGISTER, J. M. J. "Junius and Philip Francis: New Evidence." *Bulletin of the Institute of Historical Research*, 42, (1969), 158–72.

[TAYLOR, JOHN.] *The Identity of Junius with a Distinguished Living Character Established*. 2d ed. London: Taylor & Hessey, 1818. The most important single work in the search for Junius; the first argument for Philip Francis.

WEITZMAN, SOPHIA. *Warren Hastings and Philip Francis*. Manchester: Manchester University Press, 1929. An exhaustive study of their relations over Indian affairs. Strongly pro-Hastings and anti-Francis.

Index